Working with Norwegians

The guide to work culture in Norway

Sean Percival

Table of contents

Who this book is for

Expats
Non-Norwegians moving to and living in Norway

Love refugees
Recently moved to Norway for love? You're going to need a guide (and a lot of wool!)

Norwegians
Norwegians looking to better understand the challenges foreigners face when working in Norway

Corporations
As a welcome guide to new international staff working in Norway

Gifts
The ultimate gift for anyone curious about or moving to Norway

About this book

This book is your guidebook to the work culture in Norway. Here you'll find unique insights into the way Norwegians and Scandinavians do business. It is a foreigner's view packed with tips and tricks so that foreigners and Norwegians can be better at doing business together.

Be sure to visit working workingwithnorwegians.com for even more Norway work culture tips and updates. Some links found on the website and in this book may contain affiliate codes; by purchasing these products you're helping to support this book. I appreciate that, and you will too once you realize how damn expensive everything is in Norway.

For more help better understanding Norwegian work culture be sure to check out the companion book to this one, Living with Norwegians (ISBN 9788269237986). The book is available in all Norwegian book stores, or direct at the publisher's website percivalpublishing.com, and from online retailers such as Amazon.

About the author

Sean Percival is an American venture capitalist and author who should have also been successful in Norway by all accounts. However, he failed to expand a leading Silicon Valley venture fund into the Norwegian market. This was primarily due to his lack of understanding of how the Norwegian business culture differed from his own. Inspired by this failure, he collected the lessons he learned into this helpful guide. He is passionate about contributing to and fostering more collaborative business relationships in Norway.

Through his work in the Norwegian startup ecosystem these past few years, he has interacted with Norwegian businesses of all sizes and across every primary national industrial sector. Before that, he was a Vice President with Myspace and worked for several leading startups in America. His experience has shown him that businesses benefit significantly from cultural diversity and that multicultural companies are more competitive, more creative, and even have more fun.

Disclaimer for Norwegian Readers: As an American author, Sean is likely to brag excessively in a format you might not be used to. This is one of the ways our cultures are different.

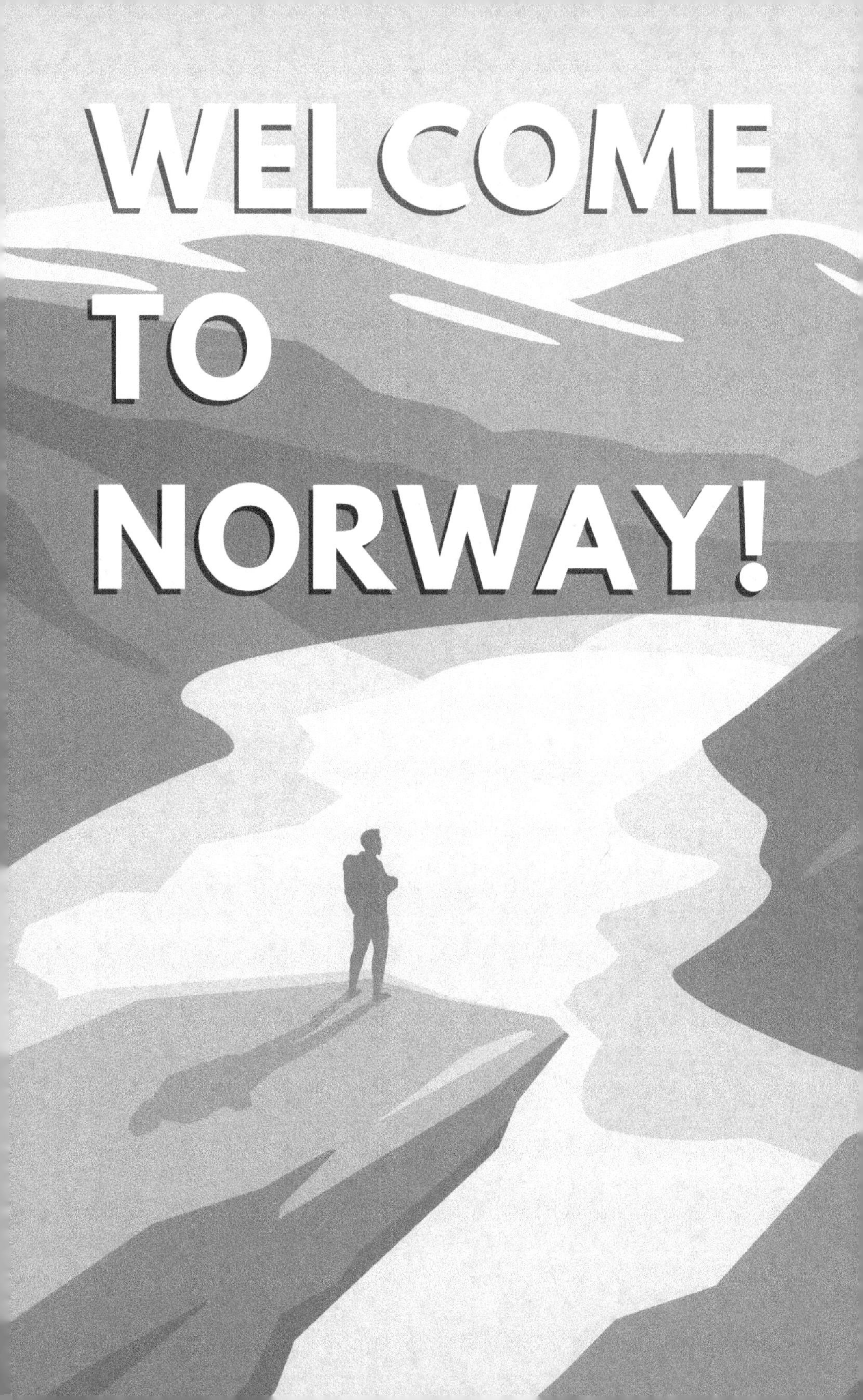

WELCOME
TO
NORWAY!

"Welcome to Norway!"

This is a phrase I often heard as I started to do business in Norway. At first, I didn't quite understand the saying, perhaps taking it too literally.

"Yes, I'm here, and thanks, I do feel welcome", I would think to myself.

Over time I would come to understand that these three simple words best captured the Norwegian experience for a foreigner like myself. For us, things are just a little different here.

"Let's go jump in that freezing cold fjord!"
—Welcome to Norway!

"It's Friday so we must make tacos!"
—Welcome to Norway!

"A popular Norwegian TV station once broadcast an entire eight-hour train ride. It was watched by millions of Norwegians".
—Welcome to Norway!

Yes, Norwegians are unique, proud, and incredibly special. The country has a rich history that includes many periods of hard times well before the good times the modern Norwegian enjoys today. This history has shaped the way Norwegian society operates. If you were to look at just about any world report on the status of the various countries, it would appear that despite some peculiar ways of doing things, everything is working very well in Norway.

The country is incredibly strong, financially, and even emotionally! Norway was in fact recently voted the happiest country in the world, even though absolutely no one ever smiles here. That might due to the one thing I've personally learned about happiness during my time in Norway: here happiness is more about being content, not overly happy or excited, just content. You're content with your job, it provides a good living. You're content with your government, they take good care of the people and can be trusted. You're content with the bus showing up on time, as it does pretty much every time. Things in Norway just work well, and the people are generally very satisfied with life here. It's almost as if each person in the entire country, in becoming equal to everyone else, has entered into a super high functioning homogeneous blob. A very good-looking blob of course. This is Scandinavia after all.

One could go on and on about all the positives of life in Norway. But this book isn't an attempt to try to sell you on the country. Chances are if you're reading this you're already here. Either you're a foreigner adapting to the Scandinavian lifestyle, or you're a Norwegian yourself, curious to get a sneak peek at how outsiders perceive you. Thankfully, you're both in the right place.

This book is instead a collection of stories and observations I've made over the years working with Norwegians. My hope is that through them, we can better understand each other and be more successful in business. Experience however has shown me that when it comes to working with Norwegians, this is not always so easy. So let this book serve as a guide from the point of view of my experience.

That experience started with my first visit to Norway, a trip that was both a mix of business and pleasure. When my feet first hit the ground here I felt something new. There was a calmness in the air together with the sometimes brutally cold weather. There was a different motion, a different flow to the city and the people that occupy it. And, like well-designed Scandinavian furniture, it was intoxicating to look at. I couldn't get enough of it really.

That first night I was incredibly lucky to have a friendly Norwegian host me for a home-cooked dinner. This was something that was fairly common in the business cultures I came from – a new business contact comes to your city for the first time so naturally you want them to feel welcome. At the time I didn't know just how rare such an invitation is in Norway, but I could tell that the way I was treated was special. Thank you, Stina, for being both an amazing and not-so-typical Norwegian.

However, in typical Norwegian style, that night went on for a long time: very, very late into the night. Lots of great food but even more drinks – this was my first experience with the aggressive Norwegian drinking culture. Before I knew it, the sun was rising, and I was stumbling home the best I could. I threw myself on the couch and fired off a text message to my boss back in America. I was incredibly excited (drunk) about the culture and business opportunities I saw in Norway:

"Hey, we should expand our business to Norway. I want to work on it".

Shortly after that, he replied: "Sure, go for it."

My boss didn't always make the best, most well-thought-out decisions, but you had to love him for his belief in his team. This is classic American risk-taking mixed with unwavering Silicon Valley optimism at its best. With that, I was already on my way to working in Norway. I knew absolutely nothing about the culture or business industries. I didn't speak Norwegian. I had for the most part no business contacts here. I did have some distant Norwegian heritage on my mother's side – that should be enough right? What could go wrong? Well, this wouldn't be a very good story if everything didn't in fact go wrong.

By all measures, I should have been successful in Norway, at least as successful as I was in America. There I was working with a leading and globally recognized Venture Fund. I had the prestigious title of "Partner" and had the ability to invest millions of dollars into businesses of my choosing. Let's just say it wasn't exactly digging a deep hole in the hot sun type of work. More like, "Yes, I'd like to upgrade to business class", and "Please, pass me the champagne" type of work.

However, my initial attempts at working with Norwegians was less about those champagne and caviar dreams—more about cold lunches and failing rather spectacularly. I butted heads with Norwegian businesses, the entire value chains from the smallest startups to the largest national institutions. And they butted back, standing their ground rather firmly.

So what happened?

For an outsider like myself, Scandinavian culture seems very approachable, inclusive even. The roots of the culture are planted clearly in equality, transparency and trust. One might assume from the outset that it would be easy to integrate quickly and easily here. However, like most significant cultures, it's incredibly nuanced. Much like an onion – with a lot of layers. Many of the layers of the Scandinavian culture are highly admirable and only a few of them just plain stink.

It's not the Norwegians' fault – I don't think they realize how they are sometimes as cold as the weather. They probably don't know how much they at times challenge a foreigner's patience. And we foreigners often take our time to truly understand and respect this culture, or any new culture. As a result, there's a lot of misalignment of experiences and expectations between both parties. That makes for much stepping on toes in the great dance that is working with Norwegians.

You'll learn about the missteps I personally made throughout this book. But despite my own failings, as I tried to work with Norwegians something happened. Like others before me, I fell in love with the country. It's not easy to love this country, you have to work hard for it. You have to struggle sometimes to be worthy of the great honor of having Norway love you back. This struggle is actually the Norwegian way.

The American way is significantly different. So many of my own challenges in Norway can be chalked up to simply being "too American". Too loud in the meeting room. Too aggressive in the deal-making. Way too optimistic in the setting of expectations. All of these are typically advantages in other business cultures but they serve as roadblocks when you work with Norwegians.

To find success here as a foreigner you need to better understand how this society operates.

So I would recommend you do as I have done. Grab a shot of the local Norwegian booze, Aquavit; put on your finest wool sweater, and double your tax liability by jumping into this beautiful country. Norway is opening up to you in its own unique way. Now more than ever, the country actually needs skilled international workers.

That's because you could say that the entire country is trying to pivot into new business and entrepreneurship. This is necessary as the price of oil continues to drop and there's a national need to strengthen business competence. However this is not something Norwegians will be able to do on their own. For proof one simply needs to look at other hubs of business innovation around the world, such as Silicon Valley, London, Singapore, and others. Those hubs are not built exclusively by locals but instead benefit significantly from international diversity. A few examples of modern American companies built by first- or second-generation immigrants are Apple, Tesla, Google, Yahoo, Intel, and Kraft Foods.

For foreigners and Norwegians to be more successful in business together, we're going to need to reduce some of the friction between our cultures. This book is my contribution to that goal. Through increased collaboration and a better understanding of our differences, I believe this to be possible.

The book is organized into several sections. It's not meant to be a concrete "dos and don'ts" guide or a heavy academic article on the intricacies of Norwegian business. You won't find any help on Norwegian business tax laws or market research reports, for example. You will, however, learn about the Norwegian values that drive business and social life. You'll receive a first-hand account of what it's actually like to work in Norway. And through reading about my own failures here, learn how to actually work with Norwegians.

My experience is of course unique, and your experience may be different. As a fair warning, you may find some stereotypes and generalizations used throughout the book. Oh, and since I'm American I'm prone to exaggerate things as well in addition to excessive personal bragging. The reality is that your Norwegian experience is what you make it. May this book serve as a guide to help you along the way. Because despite our differences, if we can better understand each other almost anything is possible. Except for maybe good weather in Oslo.

—Welcome to Norway!

VALUES

AND

CULTURE

Janteloven

One of my most jarring experiences doing business in Norway was when I first encountered the Law of Jante or Janteloven. While discussing why a Norwegian business was not excelling, a colleague of mine simply shrugged their shoulders and proclaimed, "Well, you know, Law of Jante".

Jante? What was Jante?

He sat me down for an hour and laid out a cultural anomaly that colored how almost every Norwegian (and more broadly Scandinavians) operate, both in business and in life.

The Law of Jante is a social concept created by Danish / Norwegian author Aksel Sandemose in his 1933 book A Fugitive Crosses His Tracks. You may be familiar with a similar concept used in other parts of the world called "Tall Poppy Syndrome". In Janteloven, individual success is discouraged and, in many cases, considered inappropriate. Instead, society encourages the good of the collective over any one individual. This has shaped Scandinavian culture over many years and helped to create the peaceful, modest, and homogenous society of today.

The Law of Jante

You're not to think you are anything special.

You're not to think you are as good as we are.

You're not to think you are smarter than we are.

You're not to imagine yourself better than we are.

You're not to think you know more than we do.

You're not to think you are more important than we are.

You're not to think you are good at anything.

You're not to laugh at us.

You're not to think anyone cares about you.

You're not to think you can teach us anything.

As an American born in glamorous Los Angeles, these laws were hard to grasp. My business experience was based on individuals doing nothing but telling me why they're the best! Where I come from, selling, and perhaps sometimes overselling, yourself is pretty much an art form. Los Angeles is, of course, the "Look at me!" capital of the world. Look at my fancy car! Look at my fancy house! Look at my fancy surgically-enhanced chest! More often than not, it's the boldest and the most self-congratulatory that wins. However, that's not how it works in Norway. Failing to respect the Law of Jante can dramatically decrease your likelihood of success.

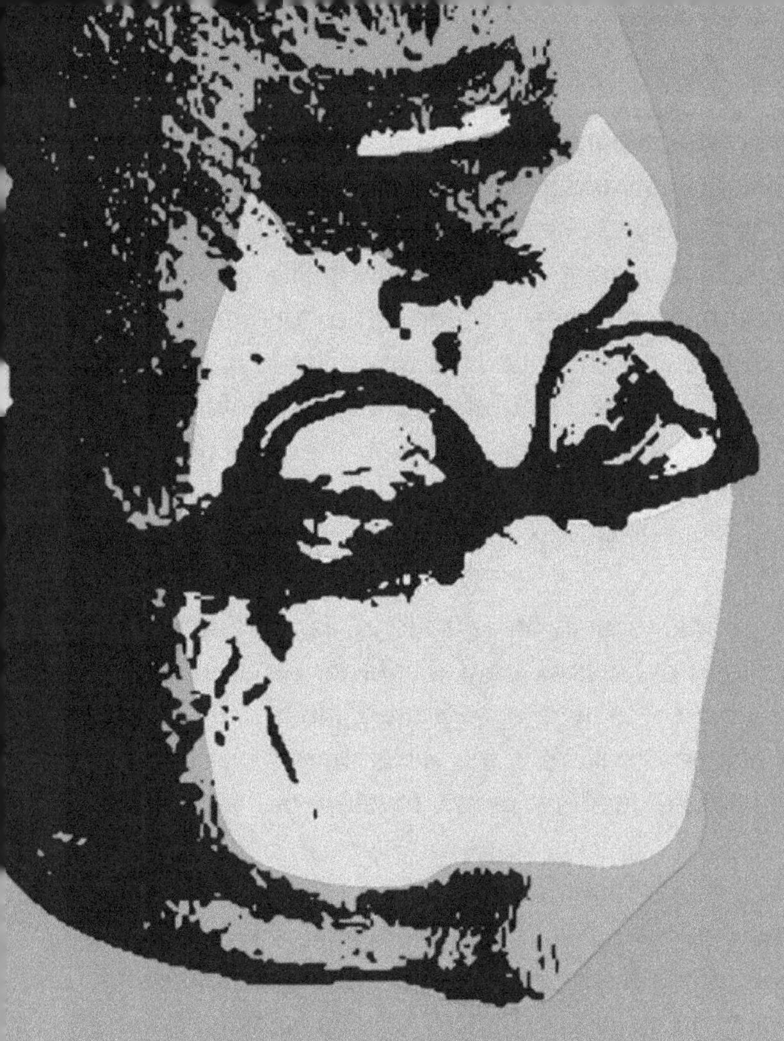

Bending Janteloven

As a foreigner who is not bridled so much by *janteloven*, you have a significant advantage in Norway. For one, you'll be allowed to get away with much more exotic behavior. Further, since Norwegians are incredibly polite, they aren't eager to interrupt someone or correct a foreigner. They understand their culture might be a bit peculiar to an outsider and therefore don't expect you always fully to conform. This allows you a few opportunities to tweak the Law of Jante. Some parts of the Law of Jante can and should be bent, and others broken entirely while you do business here.

For example, in Norwegian organizations' flat hierarchy, few are eager to lead projects or new initiatives. As an outsider, here's your chance to leverage your boldness. In almost every other business culture in the world there's no shortage of ambitious future leaders ready to step up. That's not always the case in Norway. You even have an opportunity to be slightly boastful about it as long as you follow through on what you say you'll do. This is key. Norwegians will allow for some grandstanding but completing the work and doing what you say you'll do is highly valued in this society. To be boastful or overly ambiguous but not complete will cause your colleagues to lose trust. This is a killer in Norwegian businesses.

Another example is how as a foreigner you can introduce yourself with more confidence. You can brag a little about your previous experience. As an American I can even make a cultural joke about how all we do is brag about ourselves.

Equal effort and shared praise

The Law of Jante can also impact one's ability to advance personally and be recognized within a typical Norwegian organization. To work harder or longer hours than your colleagues can easily be construed as clashing with these cultural values, which is why you don't see many overnight lights at Norwegian offices. You won't get many emails on the weekend or requests for rushed work. As a result, Norwegians enjoy some of the shortest workweeks globally with an average of just 37 hours per week. There's also heavy protection for workers in Norway to limit their hours and ensure they get ample (read "excessive") vacation time.

When you have gone the extra mile or created unique value for the company, it's usually better to recognize the team as a whole and not single out any one individual. This was a bit of a culture shock for me having worked in American and the highly competitive Silicon Valley. There, and in many other markets, personal advancement in business is governed more by what's called a meritocracy. That's to say that anyone can succeed and elevate their status high in society based solely on their merits, typically by achievements they make on their own. Along with that they are considered to be better and commonly even referred to as "the best". To achieve what they have is highly aspirational for others in the industry. This does not occur often in Norwegian business, so you have a lack of extremely high-profile business leaders for others to idolize. Instead, the praise is saved for the company they represent or the history of the brand itself as a whole. There's a much bigger focus on raising others in the organization to the same level than allowing any one individual to be raised to a disproportionate level of status. Rise up too high and society-at-large will want to push you down. If you're slipping in life, Norway is compelled to help you rise to be shoulder-to-shoulder with everyone else.

Displaying wealth

There are of course many incredibly wealthy and successful businessmen and women in Norway. Many fortunes have been made in oil, real estate, shipping and so on, although you typically won't hear about most of them. You certainly won't see many bragging about their wealth, at least not publicly. This would, of course, clash with the Law of Jante. Instead, they go to reasonably great lengths to hide that wealth, although this a somewhat futile exercise because in a country of trust and transparency, everyone's taxes are a matter of public record.

Of the 130,000+ millionaires in Norway I can think of two who could be considered 'flashy' by international business standards. They are Christian Ringnes, a beer baron, and Petter Stordalen, a hotel king and the Norwegian version of Richard Branson. They don't seem too concerned about the Law of Jante and as a result they typically throw the best parties.

Working to live, not living to work

For many Norwegians, work-life balance is incredibly important. The ideal Norwegian maintains a delicate balance in his or her life, optimizing both for efficiency and optimal relaxation time. This is best described as working to live and not living to work. The greater joy is taken in getting to the ski slopes or just enjoying a quiet evening at home with some candles lit, rather than working extra hours to advance in the workplace.

This sometimes leads to the perception that Norwegians are lazy, which is not entirely accurate. You don't often meet many lazy cultures that enjoy four-hour mountain hikes and a multitude of other types of physical punishment like cross-country skiing. The truth is more that the modern Norwegian is actually highly efficient in the workplace which makes it easier for them to put work aside and get back to enjoying life. They also take great pride in their work, so even if it takes longer to accomplish, that's perfectly alright in this society. It's better to plan to expand the time needed in all projects, just in case the sun comes out and you need to make sure you are miles away from the desk.

If you ever need a very quiet place to sit, I would recommend visiting a Norwegian office after 4pm. They are often as quiet as a soundproof library. Unlike other business cultures, there is almost no pressure in the Norwegian office to work late nights. Where I might feel guilty slipping out of work early in America for example, this is totally acceptable in Norway. It's especially true if any matters of attending to one's family are concerned, such as picking up the kids from school. However, it also applies to simply getting a head start to the winter cabin on Friday. Though when it comes to cabin culture in the workplace Norwegians often start talking about the cabin trip on Wednesday and leave as early as Thursday after lunch to beat the traffic.

There is, however, a dirty little secret among the Norwegian workforce, especially the corporate foot soldiers. Many of them will jump back online around 8pm and tend to their various work-related matters before bed, although in most Norwegian organizations it's better your colleagues don't know about your late-night keyboard cramming. It's more important to give the impression of being efficient in what you do. Achieving the desired result with the least amount of effort can earn you extra status.

So, as you do business in Norway it's important to try to avoid booking meetings too late in the day. Your attendees are likely to be eyeing the clock and anxious to get home. You'll also want to avoid trying to close deals around the many Norwegian holiday breaks and basically anytime in July and most of August. During this time the entire country has pretty much checked out and is headed to various spots around the world. Just like in the Viking days, Norwegians take great pleasure in traveling for holiday and do it as often as possible. Thanks to their strong economy and focus on quality of life, Norwegian workers receive some of the highest amounts of paid vacation days in the world.

In most cultures you're taught you need to work incredibly hard to succeed. In America and Japan you need to put in some long nights and really push yourself to get ahead. To be wildly successful, you'll need to push even harder than everyone else. Either way, you'll need to make some fairly substantial personal sacrifices to win, many times at the expense of your own health and relationships. This is especially true for foreigners who find themselves in a country other than their own. However, this is not how Norwegians see it.

Work is important, but in Norway the quality of the work is actually more important, even if that means it will take longer to complete. This keeps the stress levels for most Norwegians incredibly low. You won't find many Norwegians complaining about work stress or being overworked and stress levels are certainly much lower than what I was used to coming from fast-paced work environments like Los Angeles and San Francisco. In Norway most foreigners find they can breathe a little easier and their busy minds may slow down just a bit. This perception could also be caused by frostbite, but I'm not so sure.

That's not to say that Norwegians don't get stressed out at work, but it just might appear from an outsider's perspective they shouldn't be. After all they don't appear to be working too hard or missing any vacation. But as you work with Norwegians, and especially for those coming from highly competitive business markets, you may need to adjust your perception of the stress tolerance of others. In Norway, what might not be stressful to you may create great stress for a Norwegian. This might include things like missing a deadline, being late to a meeting or, even worse, having to share a crowded elevator with strangers. This is further compounded by Norwegians' reluctance to ask for help. Being from a proud and independent culture, Norwegians don't like to owe others or indeed have debts of any kind. This can include something as simple as getting extra help when the workload is piling up. As a foreigner you'll have to navigate when it's best to step in or identify when a colleague needs your help, as they're not likely to ask for it directly.

Some have said that work life balance is difficult to achieve in the modern age. After all, we're always just an email or Facebook notification away when needed. Norwegians, on the other hand, have done well to ensure they take ample time to shut off work and enjoy life. This usually takes the form of trips to the cabin, enjoying nature or simply getting cozy (known as getting koselig in Norwegian) at home with a nice book and the candles lit. The work will get done but not at the risk of impeding on this valuable time away from it.

For a foreigner this might be frustrating at first if you come from a fast paced work culture at home. And while it does significantly slow the development and innovation process in almost all areas of business, I recommend learning to both understand and respect it. Over time as I worked more in Norway I started to acclimatize to my surroundings here. I felt less guilty about sneaking out of the office early. I didn't check my emails for longer periods of time and I have to say, it feels pretty damn amazing. As a former ruthless capitalist, who worked far too many hours in America, I was for the first time starting to understand this whole quality of life thing. Spending a work day afternoon in the park instead of buried in my laptop unsurprisingly improved my work and even my rapport with colleagues. Instead of showing jealousy at my relaxation time, they understood. After all they would have done the same, especially on a rare day when the sun is shining here in the cold North.

Corporate Ethics

When asked about conflicts of interest John Doerr, a famous American venture capitalist, once reportedly replied "Well, no conflict, no interest". If his firm did not have a conflict, or an unfair competitive advantage, they really had no interest in the deal. This simple and short statement well encapsulates the American 'win at all costs' attitude you find in some industries. Businessmen and women in America like myself hear these war stories throughout their careers, along with grand tales of fortunes made by bending a few both ethical and legal rules. This is not the case in Norway.

Norway created the majority of its wealth on oil, something that impacts our planet negatively, yet the country highly values ethics in how it does business. This can first be seen in the large sovereign fund created by those very same oil sales. Over the years the fund has divested from any holdings that had a potential link to not-so-great things such as military weaponry, human rights violations, tobacco, and other "sin" investments. Even though the fund's performance has been stellar, they have certainly 'left money on the table' in exchange for a more ethical approach to investing. This tells you a lot about how Norway operates. The sovereign fund even has an entire team dedicated to ethics that routinely examines the business practice of the many companies they invest in.

This focus on ethics trickles all the way down into every facet of Norwegian business. This took some time getting used to. In America if we simply need to look at some of today's largest startups and we can see their origins were not always so squeaky clean. For example Airbnb, the largest provider of accommodations today, broke many rules to get where they are. They scraped data from websites, posted ads illegally to several classified services, and skirted just about

Another well-known American example is Uber, now the largest taxi company in the world in addition to being the fastest growing company of all time. To say they broke a few ethical rules is like saying the weather is only a little bit challenging in Norway. They pushed the legal and ethical envelope in almost every area of their business – from challenging the transportation laws of the cities in which they expanded to questionable international dealings with governments and law enforcement putting them in hot water with the American Justice Department. And while some of their bad behavior has recently caught up with them, investors are continuing to pour billions of dollars into the company.

Businesses like these have no chance of being created in Norway. It has actually been a challenge in my work as I push young companies and their founders to bend just about any rule to succeed. One example is pushing them to market their product in what might be described as creative ways that gently massage a few rules.

"Oh I don't know if we're allowed to do that. I wouldn't want to get in trouble", well-intentioned and ethical founder I worked with once said.

"Sounds like you would rather play it safe, even if that means going out of business in the process?" I replied, feeling extra American in saying so.

In the end this founder preferred to play it safe and not bend those rules. And in the end his business did not succeed. It's impossible to say whether he would have had a bit more bravado if he would have been more successful. But even just the thought of not playing by the rules was not something this Norwegian could entertain. Breaking the rules, especially in business, is not common in Norway. Those that do, regardless of the outcome is positive for their business, quickly lose respect in the public eye. The press seems also to take great pleasure in hanging those who do so out to dry. Unlike in America, you're not likely to get a second chance when your bad behavior becomes known. The Norwegian's memory of such bad actors lasts for as long as the fjords are deep.

Being competitive in business

Every weekday morning a highly competitive sporting event takes place in Oslo. It's not a marathon or football game. It's not even a real event to be honest, at least not an officially recognized one. However the corporate foot soldiers, especially those in the finance industry, all know about it and many of them participate as well. You've no doubt heard of the bike race the Tour de France but please let me introduce the Norwegian version, the Tour De Finance. It takes place every morning as the Norwegians living in the suburbs (*Bærum*) make their way on bicycles into the city center. But this isn't your normal morning commute.

Here on the urban grid of streets and bike paths, the Norwegian worker has the chance to do something that's more difficult to do within the office walls. That is of course to directly, and quite aggressively, compete with their coworkers and perhaps a few business competitors. When physical activity is involved then it's OK in Norway to get hyper-competitive as one does not win by simply being a slick salesperson or ruthless in business dealings. In physical competition you have to put in the work. You have to extend your own limitations and practice often. You have to take great pride in the effort to truly master it. This is what earns great respect with Norwegians. Sports, therefore, is one of the few areas that one can be super competitive in Norway. Great athletes here even reach an almost hero level of status in society.

In business it's a bit of a different story. It's not often that a Norwegian businessperson is heralded for being ruthless and decimating their competition. Even something like being a great salesperson is not well-liked here in Norway. Which was really unfortunate for me as I'm a damn good salesman! Modest as well! So I had to adjust my approach and competitive nature as I spent more time in Norway. I had to leave both my mean lawyers and handguns back in California which left me feeling unprepared on the battlefield of business in Norway.

And to Americans business really is a battle. If there's one thing American's seem to enjoy (or at least enjoy doing often) it's fight. That mentality has filtered down in how we do business as well. I first noticed the contrast between Norway and American in this regard in the very words we use in business. Our business lexicon borrows from the dictionary of war when we use words like 'beachhead' to indicate cracking open a small part of a business market before trying to expand at scale. We like to talk about 'sending in air cover' to add extra people and resources to important business deals. We love to mention how something is SNAFU (Situation Normal: All Fucked Up) or FUBAR (Fucked Up Beyond All Reason) which basically means completely fucked up. Norwegians I worked with almost never knew any of these terms. That's because business here is less about war and more about joint problem solving. Think more like NATO and less shock and awe.

In Norway you have to pick both your words and your battles wisely. There has been more than one occasion when I have failed to do so. By being too competitive and taking actions that would have earned respect back home in America (or at least created some fear in my competition), I have lost the trust of my colleagues. To show them such ruthless competitiveness only made them feel that if given the chance, I would do anything to win even if that action was at their own expense. Such selfish behavior just doesn't fly in Norway.

I have however tried to compete in the way Norwegians prefer to in the areas of sports and physical activity. This is of course a rather futile effort because when us mere mortals (non-Norwegians) compete in this regard we are at a substantial disadvantage. The combination of a few thousand hamburgers and years of the lazy American lifestyle hasn't exactly turned my body into a finely-tuned sporting machine. It's more like a big noisy diesel engine huffing and puffing as I try to keep up. Norwegians do appreciate the effort though and take some pleasure in knowing that while their business drive doesn't always match other international business cultures, they can absolutely decimate you on the cross-country skiing trails.

WORKING IN NORWAY

Inside a Norwegian office

The modern Norwegian corporate office is a thing of beauty. Imagine a vista of sensible floor plans along with that slick Scandinavian furniture in a workplace that is as efficient as the Norwegians that occupy it. Open spaces, calm colors, exposed wood and great coffee machines with touch screens make them a worker's paradise.

Like many things in Norway, much thought is put into the office design and overall experience. You won't find many dark, lifeless offices like you find throughout the world. Instead you'll find big open windows with amazing views. Even when the Norwegian worker is at the office it's important their precious nature is still within reach or at least within view.

You won't find many mazes of endless cubicles nor will you find many private offices. This isn't America where one's office sends a clear signal of your status in the company. The American executive often dreams of obtaining the coveted corner office as the ultimate symbol of status. Sometimes this even goes as far as putting the executive's office on a higher floor and overlooking the rank-and-file, lower-level employees. That is of course so they can easily survey their domain and loyal subjects. It also creates a very clear distinction of where one sits in the multi layered hierarchy of the American office place. This is less important in the flat hierarchy of Norwegian companies where they go to great lengths to avoid such perceptions of inequality.

In addition to this equality there's a calm and peace found inside the Norwegian office. However, if you ever want to cause pandemonium within these walls I recommend this one simple trick: go around and ask every single person "How are you doing!?" when you arrive in the morning. This type of pleasantry might be common in other work cultures but not so much in Norway. Instead it's more common for workers to arrive at their desk and not speak to a single soul. Norwegians are also notoriously awful making small talk as well. So if you ask how they are doing, they might even take you seriously and start telling you about all sorts of random personal issues!

Right away I noticed this is much different than a typical American office. A start of the day in USA might look more like:

9:15am
– Arrive to work (late)

9:15-9:45am
– Get coffee and engage in small talk with coworkers

9:45-10:30am
– Check Facebook and Twitter to see what coworkers and friends have posted

10:30am-11am
– Enter heated argument with coworkers about an old Game of Thrones episode

11:00am
– Start doing actual work

As you can see there's a lot of social interaction before the day really gets going. No wonder Americans have to work so many extra hours at the office! We spend our time much less efficiently. We even have what is best described as a 'water cooler culture' where employees often gather around the water cooler or coffee machine to converse extensively. Of course in Norway the water is so clean and pure that one simply needs to take it directly from the tap, no water cooler needed!

The Norwegian work day also starts significantly earlier than in other cultures, sometimes clocking in at 7:30am. In California we might come into the office as late as 10:00am, requiring us to stay much later in order to get in a proper day's work. So while many like to criticize Norwegians for leaving the office so early – typically around 4:00pm – this is not so bad when you consider how early some of them start their day.

Corporate Hierarchy

"We have a problem..." my Norwegian colleague once said to me early on a Monday morning in the office. Expecting the worst, I listened closely.

"The janitor says our team has been leaving behind too much mess in our space".

Relieved it was not a major business-related problem I shrugged it off and replied arrogantly.

"So what?"

That's when she stopped me to make sure I understood a key thing about how organizations work in Norway. You see the janitor's opinion can carry the same weight as anyone else in the organization, regardless of their title and stature. He could, like any employee, walk right into the CEO's office and voice his concerns. In Norway even large organizations are considered flat, non-hierarchical and equal. With that knowledge in hand, I was careful to be a little better about picking up after myself.

This type of flat work environment allows for open and transparent sharing of information, so everyone is included. This is counter to the organizational structure in many other regions. In other countries you have many levels of the organization and the dreaded managers-managing-managers framework. To a Norwegian, this would be considered inefficient and thus not worth doing.

Due to this flat structure it is not recommended trying a "top-down" approach to doing business with Norwegian companies.

For example, instead of trying to influence the CEO of a company to do a business deal it's better to connect directly to a specific employee in the organization. Concepts like 'going above someone's head' in an organization is highly discouraged. In fact, to approach a more senior employee and bypass someone in the organization may even be considered a great insult. The lower level employee is likely to lose trust in you, making it incredibly difficult to work together further.

Norwegian companies have bosses like anywhere else. However, their role is often much different than in other business cultures. They lead by coaching and maintaining an inclusive team environment. They don't often 'crack the whip', as we like to say in America. Instead, they work together as equals to their colleagues. And they have another important role in driving that equality. For example, if a team member is lagging behind it's the boss' job to help push them up to the same level as the rest of the team. This is counter to other cultures where a boss may focus on highlighting a single high performing individual. Ultimately managers hope that they will inspire (or intimidate) lower performing employees to step up on their own. In Norway it's more important that your team is operating at an equal level across the board.

Along with this equality you'll find the need for lots of consensus. This means that almost all company decisions will take additional time. This can be frustrating to a foreigner used to faster decision making and iteration cycles. But in Norway it's important everyone feels included. This inclusive structure makes Norwegians feel appreciated at work. As a result, they are typically incredibly loyal employees. However, it will significantly delay progress in some cases. I eventually learned to be patient and trust the process.

As a counter to this and due to lack of needing what we refer to America as 'executive buy-in' – the approval of the boss for most major initiatives – employees at all levels have a fair amount of autonomy. They are, in many cases, empowered to make their own decisions, especially as it relates to their specific job duties. This is especially true in decisions that do not require a major shift in strategy or change to the organization's structure. The classic Norwegian pragmatism strikes again.

Meeting room culture

In many other business cultures, the meeting room is often more like a battlefield. It's where ideas are pushed forward, allies are formed, and confrontation is inevitable. Those who fight well here tend to move up the executive ladder faster and get more deals done. That's not how meeting room culture works in Norway.

The Norwegian meeting room is a peaceful place, a calm room where grandstanding and chest-pounding is greatly discouraged. Even aggressive hand motions are not recommended here! This was tough for an American. I, am after, all more used to unfurling my feathers, much like a peacock, across the conference room table to make my point. However, in Norway, you don't see much peacocking in the meeting room. The scene is more similar to a flock of extremely polite songbirds chirping in agreement.
Conversations are structured and well balanced between the participants, with no single participant getting a larger share of the agenda. This happens regardless of seniority in the organization.

In the flat hierarchy of the Norwegian organization everyone has equal say. A good Norwegian boss will try to guide the conversion and let the participants work it out among themselves so it is common for them to survey the room to ask if anyone has additional thoughts on a subject. Given Norwegians' shy nature, they almost never do – or at least they feel their potentially disruptive thoughts are not worth sharing.

In Norway meetings end exactly on time and typically not a second later. This hard stop gives Norwegians a much needed exit from the room, which of course helps them avoid one of their greatest fears: having to make small talk. When the meeting ends everyone quickly shuffles out of the room. You don't linger, there is no smooth transition from meeting discussions to small talk. You sort of just look at your shoes and slink towards the exit.

Should you find yourself in the rare but difficult position of having to engage in small talk with Norwegians in a meeting room I recommend use of a few emergency conversational lubricants:

"The weather has been really awful this week right?"
(Works about 300+ days of the year)

"Wow, such amazing weather this week right?"
(Can be used once, twice if you're lucky, in the Summer)

"Have you had a chance to get to your hytte (cabin) lately?"
"I was hiking recently at (name any of the 100s of nature spots in Norway), have you ever been?"

In the most dire emergencies of small talk stalls this handy line can provide you a safe exit: "I need more coffee, bye!"

The meeting also starts exactly on time as Norwegians value punctuality. To keep a meeting attendee waiting is considered a great disrespect. Those who deliver work on time and show up for meetings on time earn extra prestige in the workplace. At the same time, arriving early to a meeting is also discouraged as this can create additional stress for the meeting host entertaining you until the meeting starts.

In general it's not appropriate to talk about one's private life during meetings in Norway. This should be avoided. From personal experience, I can recommend not oversharing about your complicated love life, that time you drank excessively and did something ridiculous, or your views on religion and politics in general. Any of those are likely to create discomfort with the meeting participants. Meetings are strictly business affairs.

It's important to know that once a decision has been made it is not to be further discussed in subsequent meetings. This is counter to many other international corporate cultures where one might try to push a previous idea forward again and again. To Norwegians, this would be considered an inefficient use of time. It's also not going to help your chances of getting your idea pushed through, as Norwegians will avoid the subject to avoid further confrontation. This was a mistake I made on several occasions. When a colleague stops returning your emails or makes great effort to avoid your presence around the office coffee machine, you have likely tried to push your own agenda too aggressively for their comfort.

With further regard to decisions being made it rarely happens at the meetings themselves, especially in an initial meeting. While most Norwegians are pragmatic people, time is usually required before a decision can be made. For large deals, expect to have to meet several times before pushing forward a proposal or contract. Norwegians actually prefer to have many meetings on a subject to ensure adequate consensus among the team members. That means there are lots of meetings in Norway. I have personally sat in on several meetings that were solely focused on planning the next meeting. Meetings within meetings may create a bit of meeting inception but it's how things get done in Norway.

Due to Nordic shyness, it may be expected for an outsider to take a more active role in the meeting room. A Norwegian colleague once candidly shared with me that they loved when there's an American in the meeting as they "provide some much needed entertainment!". We generally view meeting presentations as more theatrical opportunities to sell oneself. This does allow for a bit more exotic behavior such as telling jokes or dominating some of the conversations. For example when I first started to meet with Norwegian corporates, I was looking for their partnerships in various business efforts. Sitting at the meeting room table I often took the 'head of the table' position much like your dad might do at dinner time. I would lead the talks and outlay my entire presentation before soliciting for questions at the end. I was given more allowance to do this as a foreigner but it was still important to provide others time to speak. You may need to poke them to do so several times as they are not likely to interrupt you.

In these cases, it may be OK to break standard Norwegian meeting room culture. Just don't push your luck and look for the opaque signals that tell you when it's time to get back on track. These signals include Norwegians breaking eye contact, excessively sipping their water or coffee or a nervous tapping of one's pen. To an outsider these subtle signals may be hard to detect at first so as you work for Norwegians it's best to fine tune yourself to detect discomfort in a room.

Finally you may notice a Norwegian meeting room looks a lot like your grade school classroom at times. Since Norwegians are extremely polite and not eager to interrupt a speaker they instead raise their hand when they wish to talk, just like the classroom. This was a bit silly to me at first as in the American meeting one simply interjects into a conversion when someone has completed their thought or speaks louder than others to get their word in. This type of aggressive jockeying for attention does not happen in the peaceful Norwegian meeting room, however. Norwegians will often hold up one finger to add a comment to an existing conversion or two fingers when raising a new subject. Very efficient!

Understanding Norwegian meeting room best practices is very important to adapting to working with Norwegians. As this is the primary vehicle for advancement of both your own work-related initiatives and earning personal status in the workplace. Whenever in doubt of the status of a project or to clarify something with a colleague one simply needs to call for a meeting.

Or, as Norwegians do, call for a meeting to plan that meeting!

The foods of Norwegian business

I once took an early morning meeting at the gleaming and massive Telenor (Norway's largest telecom provider) campus. As I was shuffled through the corporate maze of desks and endless hallways and eventually to a conference room, something was waiting for me there on the table. It was a small arrangement of waffles, brown cheese, and jam next to a pot of coffee.

"Ohhhhh you must be someone important for them to have ordered this!" remarked the corporate foot soldier with me.

This struck me as a bit of an odd statement. After all the Telenor executives had called for the meeting with me and it was of some potential significance (we eventually worked on a deal for approximately $1M USD). Why was them going to the extra effort to provide food notable? And we aren't exactly talking about the royal spread here! Someone mixed some flour and milk together to make a waffle and said here's the best we got. OK... Upon closer inspection, I noticed they didn't even slice the cheese for us! We had to do it ourselves using some type of Viking cheese slicer.

—Welcome to Norway!

In many other business cultures you tantalize and amaze your business contacts with a veritable cornucopia of treats. From pastries to sandwiches, to sushi, and of course the American doughnut. I once continued meeting with a Silicon Valley startup not for the business opportunities, but simply because they always had the best flakey French croissants at their meetings. Norwegians however share and appreciate food differently, especially in business.

This is driven much by Norway's history with food. Prior to the oil boom Norway was historically a rather poor country so having food was not about enjoyment but more about plain survival. While times have certainly changed economically these humble food traditions have remained. The waffles in the Telenor conference are a perfect example of this and they can even be considered a luxury for Norwegians. Beyond the flour and milk a simple item like this is considered to be 'made with love' and the waffles carry that love throughout their delicious crevices. So what I perceived as a low budget snack was actually a symbolic gesture of my importance as their guest. They appreciated me, it was just easier for them to show it through waffles than to have to say it verbally. It was very Norwegian, actually.

The Norwegian business lunch is fairly unremarkable with little fanfare. Since the typical Norwegian office is more about efficiency lunches are meant to be quick (usually just 30 minutes). They also typically start at 11:30am, slightly earlier than most other business cultures. So by noon you're already done and back to work. Lunch is also not meant to be enjoyable but instead you just need it to survive. The polar opposite of this would be the French business lunch which can run two hours and might even include some wine. Drinking during a Norwegian business lunch is not typical and would likely be considered inappropriate. Norwegians in general like to save their drinking for the evening, times they need to be social, and of course when they are trying to get laid.

For lunch cold sandwiches are often on the menu and warm lunch is not always available, which is strange in a country so cold you think you would find more items to warm one's tummy. Once again, it comes down to food as more of a means for survival. It's also about being practical and fast so that you can get back work. All that being said, lunches are in most cases very healthy. You might lose some weight in Norway and be more healthy. I know I shed a few kilos simply by avoiding the sugary foods often found in the American lunch. No wonder everyone in Norway is in such good shape.

You typically don't go out for lunch in the Norwegian workplace. That might be considered an inefficient use of time, plus food is so damn expensive. Employees sometimes bring in their own lunch wrapped in wax paper (*matpapir*). They bring mostly sandwiches of the open face variety. Many companies also offer a cafeteria (or *kantine* as it's called in Norway.) Here you should be expected to bus your own tray and clean your plate. Everyone in the corporate cafeteria is an equal and it's common to see the CEO dining here right alongside the rank-and-file employees. He or she will also bus their own plate just like everyone else. That famous Norwegian equity even comes down to doing the dishes.

WAFFLES

Similar to Belgium waffles, Norwegian waffles are the Scandinavian version so they are of course much thinner and better looking than their heavy Belgian cousins. In the boardroom or by the campfire, these are always a hit. Slap a slice of *brunost* (brown cheese) and a dab of jam to get the full experience. No syrup is required.

BRUNOST (BROWN CHEESE)

As a newcomer to Norway many locals will ask if you've had the *brunost* yet and what you think of it. So it's best to quickly try it and get that out of the way. I think many Norwegians enjoy offering *brunost* as a cruel trick, the classic "let's make the foreigner try our strange food" gag. However many (myself included) find *brunost* to be quite tasty. It's high in sugar and it is like cheese so as an American that's pretty much our two main food groups. While technically not cheese it's more of a byproduct of cheese production itself. Most countries would throw it out but during Norway's more humble and poorer times they added sugar to provide additional food for the people. So *brunost* is considered an important part of cultural identity for Norwegians.

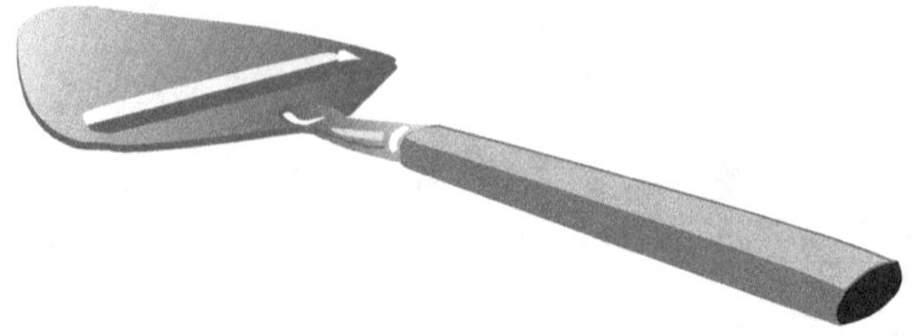

THE CHEESE SLICER

Accompanying the *brunost* you're likely to find a Viking cheese slicer. This utensil was invented by Norwegians and they're quite proud of that. Mastering the art of a good slice will also help to score status points with your Norwegian colleagues. The trick is to grab the cheese firmly and pull the slicer towards you in a smooth motion. Keep the slicer level to avoid 'canoeing' the cheese, an obvious giveaway that you're a foreigner.

COFFEE

Scandinavians, in general, drink a lot of coffee and rank among the top consumers per capita. They tend to take it black without milk which is perhaps another indicator of Norway's more modest economical past where milk was a bit of a luxury. For cultures where it's more common to mix coffee with milk or cream, you'll need to request it. You might also not always find your fancy espresso and cappuccino options you find in other offices around the world. Norway is also one of the few corners of the world where you won't find many Starbucks. Instead, search out an Espresso House or Kaffebrenneriet for your coffee business meetings.

Working in
a shy
country

The scene: 3am at a McDonald's in Oslo. I had just attended a business event and survived the Norwegian drinking culture. Now it was time to do something we Americans do best: eat a big greasy cheeseburger.

With me were several new Norwegian business contacts I had been in discussions with over the last few months. In their well-lubricated state the shyness was gone and thus they eagerly asked:

"So have you ever been cross-country skiing?!"

As I daydreamt about the burger on its way, I thought well I've been 'normal' skiing many times but I have no idea what cross-country skiing actually is. It sounds like a lot of work, to be honest.

"No..." I replied simply.

"Oh, then you must join us! It's amazing! We'll trek for hours in the freezing snow, take a break to eat a candy bar, and then return!" They explained with much excitement in their eyes.

To me this sounded like an awful way to further get to know each other. How could we work on our business partnership while skiing in a straight line, in the middle of the woods, in total silence? I was not incredibly eager to accept and follow up on their invitation. This was a big mistake on my part, and as a result the business relationship did not go much further.

What I had missed was that for Norwegians an activity like cross country skiing is how business relationships are strengthened. We do a physical activity together and that usually includes some element of suffering or hard work and then after that we can begin to build trust together. You have to first put in the work to build a solid foundation for your working relationship.

This is counter to many other business cultures where you would first enjoy something nice like a fancy dinner or entertainment event as the basis of your future business dealings. That's not how it works in Norway. In fact, if you try to woo Norwegian business contacts in this manner they will assume you want some type of favor. That may make them reluctant to work with you further. Be careful not to wine and dine your new relationships too extravagantly at first as you might do around the world. In other words, save the blow out Las Vegas trip and luxury box seats at the sporting event until the relationship has been well-established.

One wonderful example of suffering through physical activity that – surprise! – involves more skiing is the *Birkebeinerrennet*. It's an annual 54 km cross-country ski race ending in beautiful Lillehammer. As a foreigner, you would earn extra status in the business community having completed this race. Many CEOs at the major Norwegian corporations participate at some time as an almost rite of passage. Their peers value their dedication to training and that admiration spills over into the workplace.

When I first came to Norway I actually purchased a pair of cross country skis, as one does. However, to be perfectly honest, they have sat in the corner of my apartment for several seasons, unused.

Having failed to take advantage of several good opportunities to utilize them and further a business relationship they continue to collect dust. Perhaps I'm saving them for that really important business deal. That said if you're slightly healthier than me then come and borrow my skis. This is your best opportunity to establish a relationship and perhaps even make a new friend in Norway.

Yes, the rumors are true. Norwegians are notoriously difficult to get to know. Your typical Norwegian is much like a coconut, with an extremely hard shell yet a soft and gooey inside. But how does one access the softer inside?

Back in America, work is life and your work life often intersects with your social life. However, in Norway these two are distinctly separate. They exist independently without much overlap, thus making it even more difficult to build relationships both personal and professional. Even after several years of working in Norway I have exactly zero extremely close relationships, either business or personal, at least to the level of what I had back in America. This makes those cold winters especially tough. As a foreigner I can give you only one piece of advice to find a shortcut to getting close: look to other expats who are likely in a similar situation as yourself. Misery loves company, as they like to say.

Another opportunity to make both business and personal relationships happens outside the sphere of work. You do this by participating in '*dugnad*' or community work like cutting trees, cleaning streets or other volunteer activities. There is some expectation by society that you'll participate in these routines. No wonder everything is always so clean in Norway.

ETIQUETTE AT WORK

Using titles and first names

As you start to work in Norway, you'll notice things are a bit different with regard to names. First of all, there aren't that many unique names in Norway. This reminds me of the time when a colleague was trying to remember a business contact whose name starts with "J." I responded, "I know 10 people named Johan, 6 people named Jonas, and 5 more guys named Jonah", which didn't help us remember. So, while working with Norwegians, you won't have to remember too many distinctly unique names. You will, however, have enough challenges keeping them all straight and matched to the right people.

In Norway, titles are also not used very often as most business environments are casual in nature. Additionally, to use flashy titles as a means of impressing colleagues is discouraged, lest anyone individual try to assert themselves as more important in the organization. Yes, I'm talking to you Brad Braderson, Senior Vice President of Regional Sales and New Product Development Asset Manager. In Norway, you're just Brad and that's perfectly all right. Save the long titles for the business card. Although, many Norwegians go as far as to even exclude their titles on their business cards, at least the Norwegian version of it. This can even apply to using distinguished titles such as Doctor, depending on the social setting. Much of this is because Norway is a very egalitarian society that never had an aristocracy. Those fancy people lived in Stockholm or Copenhagen. The last lordship in Norway (The Count of Jarlsberg) lost his title in 1829 and that was the end of that. For a quick tip, it's best to simply listen to how Norwegians introduce themselves to figure out how they wish to be identified.

For foreigners, you want to also be careful about speaking of your current or past accolades as it pertains to titles. Back home in America, it was more common for me to say I was CEO of this and Vice President of that. I would typically use my past titles to help sell my authority and experience, but this is less desirable in Norway. As I gave public presentations, I even had an entire slide dedicated solely to my past experience. However, as I worked more and more in Norway that slide gets used much less often. Even though as a foreigner you're allowed to get away with just a tad more bragging about your past experience. Like most things in life, it's better to do it with some moderation in Norway.

Of course, to the international business community, titles and the weight they carry is much more important. This may cause some communications from Norwegians to appear cold or even show a lack of respect. This, in addition to the direct (Norwegians would say efficient!) way they communicate, can cause some awkward back and forth. Over time I've learned to put some of my ego aside and embrace the straightforward approach they take. You may find like I have, that it is in fact a more efficient approach to building a relationship, and of course being Norway, it's the more fair and egalitarian approach.

Both in business and in personal interactions it is best to avoid using "Mr.", "Mrs." and "Miss" courtesy titles. This is considered too formal in almost every type of setting. Also, in Norway one's personal relationship status is not really the business of others. Thanks to a strong and equal social welfare system, many couples are together for many years without formally marrying. It's best to avoid potentially "miss"-identifying a colleague's or business partners' marital status and risking embarrassment.

Sometimes a Norwegian's name consists of two names, for example, Per Martin. You would normally never shorten this to something like just "Per". Instead, always use their full name in all of its intended Norwegian glory. Again, look to see how they introduce themselves to you and others. If they use the full "Per Martin", so should you. Over time, as you strengthen your relationship with Norwegians, you might be able to use more casual nicknames or in this example, something like "PM". This can be helpful for us foreigners who struggle with some pronunciation issues of the more complex and longer Norwegian names you often find.

There's a bit of an insider joke in Norway when it comes to names as well. If one wants to show more class they simply move the hyphen from between their first two names to between their last two surnames. Personally, I don't know why anyone needs more than one name, but in Norway this is one example where excess is OK.

One exception where titles are required is when referring to the members of the royal family of Norway. Even in an extremely egalitarian culture, it's good to be king! They are always referred to as "King", "Queen", "Crown Prince" and "Crown Princess". If you're lucky enough to speak directly to the royal family, you would address the King and Queen as "Your Majesty" and "His or Her Royal Highness" in the case of the Crown Prince and Crown Princess respectively. They also require more formal introductions for example, "His Royal Highness Crown Prince Haakon..." I was actually lucky enough to meet the Crown Prince for an intimate breakfast at his home, the Skaugum Estate, and I was incredibly nervous about the event. We Americans don't have much experience with nobility. You could even say we've spent the last 200+ years moving away from the concept altogether.

Still, such a title demands a serious amount of respect that I was ill-prepared for. Do I bow? Do I kiss the ring? Does he greet me by touching a sword to both shoulders? I was unsure. However, the experience proved to be surprisingly casual. Despite their high stature and exclusive use of titles, even the royal family in Norway is incredibly approachable and treated similarly to the population at large.

This wasn't always the case in Norway; as recently as the 1970s, titles were used throughout the country. This included in business, noble families and included professional titles like Doctor. Although as the society enjoyed its new financial prosperity during the time, the focus quickly shifted towards the more egalitarian approach we see today throughout Scandinavia. Personally, I don't think their usage has been missed and even my big American ego has learned to accept it. Although, I still keep my title on my business cards. In bold. Maybe in a slightly larger font. Some old habits are hard to change, after all.

Who's paying for dinner?

I made a serious gaffe in one of my early visits to Norway. I had asked a colleague to assemble a dinner with influential players in my industry. My goal was nothing more than a casual setting to get to know each other and for me to explain the new work I was doing in the region. Even though I specifically said ahead of time the dinner would "be my treat", panic ensued when the bill came I swiftly swiped my credit card covering the entire bill. Once finished I turned around to see a look of shock and uncomfortableness upon their faces. I had made a huge mistake and there was no going back now. A wonderful night of getting to know my new business contacts quickly turned into an awkward moment for everyone.

Before I could swipe my card with the speed of fine dining ninja there was some polite protesting and insistence on covering their own meals. However, I waved those off, assuming it was a general courtesy that one often does. You offer to pay once or twice and eventually relent, letting the other person pick up the tab. All the while I was not truly understanding the uncomfortable position I had put my dinner guests in.

You see, in Norway, there really is no such thing as a free meal. And that's too bad, as you'll soon find out that food in Norway is incredibly expensive! To buy someone a meal, even in a business setting, is often construed as you trying to win favor. You can imagine how this might complicate dating life in Norway for a foreigner! This is a culture that does not want debts or the feeling that something is owed to anyone. They value their independence and have fought hard (and fought off several invasions) to keep it. So, you have to be mindful of your wining and dining as you do business in Norway.

Additionally, there are even further tax repercussions in these scenarios. In a country where they love their taxes, there is little affordance for gifting, free meals or other questionable business expenses. One could easily get in trouble for accepting too many gifts and meals. And you, as the giver, are also limited to what is considered an appropriate business expense. For example, buying a colleague a glass of wine is probably OK, but an expensive dinner and several bottles of wine is probably not. This is contrary to many other Western and European business expense rules. In those markets, one might be more prone to going slightly overboard knowing that both the company is paying and probably writing it off as a business expense. In American business culture, it's even a bit of a joke one might make while covering a huge bill. Proclaiming "tax write off!" as they eagerly swipe the corporate credit card. In Norway it's not really a joking matter. And in the name of transparency, which this country loves, you may have to record who attended a business dinner and even what was discussed. This makes me hope none of my bad or inappropriate dinner jokes made the official records.

When it comes to buying dinners or other business-related perks, I've come to learn that Norwegians have a very broad definition of corruption. This is for several reasons but primarily comes down to Norwegians not wanting to feel indebted to anyone. When they do, they'll be eager to pay off any debts quickly, as having this debt hanging over them will create great stress and anxiety. One has to be super careful about not offering too much at first when building a new business or personal relationship in Norway, as you can literally lose them through your generosity, even if your intentions are not to win influence.

So, in Norway don't feel an overwhelming pressure to buy business contacts dinners as you might feel in other business cultures around the world. As the waiter comes to your table they will typically first ask if they should split the bill. Instead of using this moment to show off your credit card prowess, take a moment to read the vibe from your dinner companion(s). If they insist on splitting, it's better to offer little protest and avoid being overly insistent on covering the bill.

When it comes to buying dinners or other business-related perks, I've come to learn that Norwegians have a very broad definition of corruption. This is for several reasons but primarily comes down to Norwegians not wanting to feel indebted to anyone. When they do, they'll be eager to pay off any debts quickly, as having this debt hanging over them will create great stress and anxiety. One has to be super careful about not offering too much at first when building a new business or personal relationship in Norway, as you can literally lose them through your generosity, even if your intentions are not to win influence.

Dressing like a Norwegian

By European standards especially, but even by American standards, Norwegian business dress code would be considered informal and casual. In Norway it's less important to display one's wealth through fashion as you might see elsewhere. Or at least, you typically do not do it at the workplace. In fact, wearing exotic or ostentatious outfits is usually discouraged in a business setting. Heaven forbid one stands out and attempts to bend the Law of Jante with a fabulous neckline.

Men typically wear conservative business suits in most industries: blazer and trousers with no tie. In some industries like finance and sales, a more formal suit and tie may be appropriate. In either case, it's important the suit is well-tailored. In fact, the only colleagues I see wearing a sloppy, ill-fitting suit are typically other Americans. They end up standing out like a sore, poorly-dressed thumb among the well-tailored lines of their Norwegian counterparts.

Thrown over the shoulder of these nice suits, you'll notice Norwegian businessmen tend to opt for a simple backpack (locally called a rucksack) instead of a traditional briefcase or more fashionable bag. While the juxtaposition of the nice crisp suit and floppy bag was a bit strange to me at first, I now understand. It's just more practical and in Norway, practicality usually wins. In other parts of the world this is sometimes known as function over fashion, or form follows function, which is, as it turns out, the mantra for almost all Scandinavian design.

For women in most industries, a well-tailored dress, trousers or pantsuit works just fine. For jewelry, it's usually minimal and understated. Stiletto high heels are usually reserved for evening receptions only. In fact, even shoes that make noise when walking are socially discouraged! They may make others believe that the person wants to attract attention, again against the Law of Jante. Besides, a pair of nice heels, as sexy as they might be, are not extremely practical for walking around Norway's uneven and sometimes slippery sidewalks. So, women's shoes, like men's, are usually not very elegant or fashionable. You may notice as I have, that Norwegian women don't look entirely comfortable in heels. A lack of practice in them perhaps over the years has not given them the ability to slink and sway as elegantly as women in other parts of the world. Footwear, like many things, are more about being practical. Hats are not very common unless it's for keeping your head warm during the wintertime.

All of this is not to say that Norwegians don't appreciate fashion! In fact, they dress very well and purchase a lot of clothing from their slightly more fashion-savvy neighbor Sweden. I recall meeting a few Swedes once who all were impeccably dressed to the point of being ready for the fashion week catwalk. Curious, I asked them what they all did for a living. They replied they were accountants which caused me to pause and think of my accountant back home in America. His outfit of choice was a worn-out dress shirt that had been through the washing cycle a few too many times yet still managed to keep a few noticeable stains, along with some frayed edges. Just then I realized my wardrobe was not even close to being at the same high level as a Scandinavian accountant.

You'll also notice Norwegians incorporate a lot of black and dark colors into their outfits, enough to make even a high school goth kid jealous. The typical Norwegian outfit may consist of black on black on black with a splash of grey. This is actually part of the overall Scandinavian fashion aesthetic. Many have tried to explain why but it probably comes down to the fact that tall gorgeous blonde people simply look fabulous in all black.

If you're coming from a warmer region (so about 90% of the planet) please allow me to introduce you to your new best friend... wool! This tried and true material is your key to surviving the cold Norwegian winter. Sometimes referred to by Norwegians as 'super underwear', these butt warming, life-saving garments are super indeed. Be sure you don't go for some less expensive wool and polyester blend. Get the good stuff, that full wool. Your legs and booty will thank you; I promise.

Wool is actually very fashionable in Norway as well! The brand you choose to wear when you go to a sporting event will send a subtle signal about your social status. The more expensive the wool, the higher your social status. In case you're wondering, the best wool is Merino wool, or if you're really fancy, a cashmere and silk mix. You won't have to worry about itchy fabric with these options, as they are incredibly soft.

The same goes for the sport outfit itself. You will often see Norwegians walking around town in very expensive sport outfits, as this is how Norwegian show status through clothing. When it is done during a sport or physical activity context it is allowed. It is also allowed in the office, for example, on a Friday when you plan to head right to the cabin (hytte) after work.

Norwegians, much like many Asian cultures, remove their shoes at the door. This is especially true in the winter time when your shoes may be covered with snow and wet mud, although it applies to the entire year. For foreigners, this might be a bit strange as you attend work related social events at a colleague's house. Don't be too surprised to see a house full of Norwegians, dressed rather well in suits and dresses, yet all standing there in their socks. It is not common to remove your shoes in the workplace, although I've seen it as a company policy. If you see the same this is a great chance to joke, "Wow, this office is *very* Norwegian!".

So that's pretty straightforward right? Norwegian women own plenty of amazing, high-end clothes, they simply rarely wear them. Men wear ties but no shoes to parties and don't wear ties to work.

—Welcome to Norway!

Norwegian drinking culture

In most business cultures there's some element of drinking related activities. "Work hard, play hard", as we like to say back in America. However, in Norway drinking culture may come as a bit of a surprise to foreigners. That surprise may also consist of waking up in a hung-over daze, partially dressed and for some still unexplained reason, even to this day, covered in glitter and what appeared to be kebab sauce. To say Norwegians don't party hard would be like saying the tax is only a little high in Norway. It would be quite an understatement. No, in fact, Norwegians enjoy a drink (or fifteen) and those drunken adventures often cross over into business life as well. With the cost of alcohol in Norway so high, there's a local expression that covers their approach to drinking quite well "being half drunk is a waste of money". In Norway they don't go halfway when it comes to drinking, more like all the way and then some.

One of my first experiences with Norwegian drinking culture was after attending a business conference in Oslo. With the work day done and sights set on enjoying the evening, we set out not to a bar, but to a local resident's house. Thus began the Norwegian pre-party, or as it's known in Norway, the *vorspiel*. This is a critical launching off point for an evening of festivities. It was told to me then that because of the high cost of alcohol in Norway it's a common practice. One must try to get as loaded as possible beforehand at home to avoid racking up a sky-high bill at the bar. Over time I also realized that when it comes to extended social efforts, Norwegians usually needed a few drinks to get started. It allows them to loosen up a bit and be open to doing really crazy things, like talking to a stranger. To get to this point that means a pre-party can actually go on fairly long, without venturing out until well past midnight.

Bars and nightlife in Norway are typical to what you might find in other European cities, just significantly more expensive. Due to this high cost, there is no expectation for you to buy drinks for your colleagues, although you'll usually be able to pick up one round for the group without too much protest. Otherwise, everyone is expected to be self-sufficient when it comes to lubricating oneself. For the reasons above, it's also uncommon to find an 'open bar' at either work or social events. Tipping the bartender is also not required or expected in Norway, as service workers make a living wage even without your tips.

As we ventured from bar to bar and from club to club that evening, I started to make some new friends within our group. This is a side effect of a well-oiled-up Norwegian. They actually want to talk and get to know you! Here's your chance to dramatically reduce the time it takes to build a closer relationship with your colleagues and Norwegian business partners. The hard exterior that most Norwegians wear cracks in this moment and new bonds and trust can be established, granted you both are able to remember the connection (and any of the evening's drunken activities) the following day.

I made another new friend that night, who goes by the name Aquavit, the local Norwegian liquor that is similar to schnapps. As a foreigner you'll most certainly be encouraged to try it even though most Norwegians seem to hate it. And for good reason: it tastes a bit like old shoe combined with spicy cough medicine, so the first shot is likely to be brutal. It will, however, earn you respect among your Norwegian colleagues with every gulp. After indulging a few more shots, you may actually find you enjoy the stuff like I did.

That night and far too many shots later, the evening started to creep into the next morning. But the fun is not over yet in Norway: as I squinted my eyes hoping to find a taxi and my escape, a new friend put their arm around me and excitedly asked:

"Have you ever been to a real Norwegian nachspiel? No? Then you must come!"

Not knowing what I was agreeing to, we were now on to the final journey of a common Norwegian night of drinking. The 'nachspeil', or the after party. At this point it's getting late, or early the following day, depending on how you look at it. It's too late to buy alcohol anywhere so you head back to someone's apartment to raid whatever is left there. This is the point of the night where things are best described as "getting sloppy" or borderline absurd. Everyone has had far too much to drink and it's a bit of last man or woman standing. If you're a foreigner that probably won't be you, as Norwegians have great stamina in the arena of marathon drinking. If you're lucky enough to make an early exit, try to sneak out quietly. Otherwise you risk having to take a "penalty shot" for your early departure, one final shot of Aquavit for the road.

Even though alcohol is a much-needed social lubricant in Norway, the distribution of it is highly regulated and restricted, perhaps to help ensure Norway remains a quiet, safe and homogenous society. As your friendly Loud American and free market capitalist here, I can't help but wonder if this strict alcohol control is a major driver of the heavy Norwegian drinking culture. As humans we often want more of what we cannot have. So, when it's available and appropriate, it might be fair to say Norwegians go a bit overboard.

They also do this during the rare moments the sun comes out by soaking up as much as possible.

Drinking culture starts at a very young age for Norwegians. Unlike other European or Latin cultures, it's considered highly unacceptable to give minors alcohol in a dinner or social setting. That doesn't stop them from starting early in life, however. And it usually continues throughout early adult life with much of the Norwegian college experiences being centered around drinking. There's also a fair amount of social pressure to drink in Norway both in business and personal settings. I like to joke that both my tax rate and alcohol consumption has doubled since I moved here.

Norwegians young and old also tend to use drinking games as means of socialization. This gives them an easy framework for interacting with each other. That really helps as one waits for the drinks to kick in and more fluid social engagements can emerge. It's also one of those rare moments when you can engage in some friendly competition with your colleagues. Excelling at trivia, for example, can earn you extra prestige with Norwegians.

You can purchase beer at most grocery stores but only until 8pm during the week, 6pm Saturday, and not at all on Sundays. To get the good stuff, you'll need to visit a state-run *Vinmonopolet*, or the wine monopoly. Here, similar hours apply, but one can also purchase wine, Prosecco, and hard liquor (also known as the good stuff). Be sure to plan ahead for your work and social events in Norway. Failing to load up on alcohol ahead of time might leave you with very few options and worst of all, a rather boring event.

As you attend or host parties in Norway you may also notice things work a bit differently here with regard to sharing of booze. In many other cultures, it would be common to bring a bottle of wine for the host and everyone to share. However, due to the cost of alcohol in Norway, and Norwegians not wanting to owe others, most gatherings follow a strict BYOB (Bring Your Own Booze) policy. So as a foreigner you should not expect to have a drink served to you upon arrival as you find in many other cultures. Norwegians may also remember you did not bring your own alcohol and probably feel unhappy about it. Of course, they won't say anything about it, but they'll do what they do best in awkward social situations, silently protest it in their own heads.

Perhaps most important to know in Norwegian drinking culture is how to toast your colleagues and all the new intoxicated friends you'll be making. Grab your favorite drink, raise it up high (although still below your nose) and at any time proclaim "*skål!*" (pronounced "skol") loudly. The word comes from the Norwegian word for skull, and hails back to Viking times when it was customary to drink from the skull of your enemy. It is also considered good manners to stare into the eyes of your companions while you toast in Norway. It may be one of the few chances to do such a thing with a shy Norwegian, so enjoy it.

The apex of Norwegian drinking culture, at least as it pertains to the workplace, is *Julebord*, or the Christmas party. A year's worth of pent up work frustrations is released on this glorious night. It's a bit of a fancy night, at least fancier than a typical Norwegian event. Often taking place in a luxury hotel or other fine establishment, this is one night of the year when it's OK to indulge a little (more like a lot). You've almost made it through the brutal winter so perhaps you've earned it after all.

Julebord etiquette

The apex of Norwegian drinking culture, at least as it pertains to the workplace, is *Julebord*, or the Christmas party. A year's worth of pent up work frustrations is released on this glorious night. It's a bit of a fancy night, at least fancier than a typical Norwegian event. Often taking place in a luxury hotel or other fine establishment, this is one night of the year when it's OK to indulge a little (more like a lot). You've almost made it through the brutal winter so perhaps you've earned it after all.

And indulge the typical Norwegian does at *Julebord*. The night is full of lots of great food, comfort food, along with songs, dancing and often a comedian or other form of entertainment. However, much of the indulgence takes the form of consuming a large amount of alcohol. A table setting might include beer and wine, and of course, Aquavit. As you can imagine, these events can go on well into the night.

Much has been said and debated about *Julebord*, but most Norwegians seem to take the Las Vegas approach: what happens at *Julebord*, stays at *Julebord*. In Norway, there are so many social codes that must not be broken. However, on this wonderful night of the year, many of those rules fly out the window. You can be a little more wild than usual. You can say a few inappropriate things. You can sleep with your colleagues, even if he or she is married! All that really matters is that you don't talk about it the next day at the office, which should be pretty easy to do in the already quiet Norwegian office.

Sleeping with Norwegians

—

While working in Norway you're going to want to sleep with Norwegians, and that's perfectly alright! After all, Norway's greatest importer of foreigners is not through immigration or job placements, but through love itself. And there is no shortage of ridiculously good-looking people to fall in love with here, even if that's just for one night.

As a foreigner you'll often be asked, "So, what brought you to Norway?" or the more direct, "Why Norway?". In many cases this will be the first question they ask. Norwegians are eager to ask foreigners this question because they are almost always expecting you to say because of love. While Norway is a vibrant country full of many opportunities many Norwegians struggle to understand why a foreigner would come here. It is of course not typically because of the amazing weather or low cost of living.

If you moved to Spain or France, you are far less likely to get asked this question as often as one does in Norway.

In a business setting, this can be problematic. If you begrudgingly respond that "Yes, I'm here for love". That can actually have a negative impact on your perception from others. I think it's partially related to giving the appearance of being too cliché, but in some cases that your own commitment to Norway is not tied to the society as a whole, but only to a single individual Norwegian. You'll have to work extra hard to show your appreciation for Norway and respect to the entire country and its history. I also think that Norwegians view their people (especially the very good-looking ones) as a finite resource. They are therefore not super-excited about a bunch of foreigners swinging in and taking them off the market. Their ancestors, after all, worked hard to drag (literally) the best-looking people from around Europe back to Norway during their many Viking conquests.

If you are however lucky enough to sleep with a Norwegian, or two, or twelve during your business adventures, there are a few social norms to understand. The first is that casual sex is fairly prevalent both in Norway and throughout the Nordics. So slow down there, tiger, and try to avoid falling too head over heels in love after just a single hot night under the sheets. There's a high likelihood that the experience, as passionate as it might have been, is taken less seriously by your Norwegian partner. In the case of sleeping with coworkers and then sitting across from them at the meeting room table the next day at work don't be too surprised if their demeanor has switched right back to work mode. That may have been a one-time performance. Unless of course, you get lucky again at next year's *Julebord* when you're both enjoying yourself a little too much.

Still, when the moment has passed don't be too surprised if it's never mentioned again.

Secondly, since there is a strong separation between work and social life, it's important those hot romps away from the office don't interfere with office life itself. In an incredibly equalitarian business culture, it's important someone is not given special treatment at work, regardless of how good they might be in bed. To show an unfair bias or give someone favorable treatment at work because of a personal relationship is a big no-no. Sleeping your way to the top doesn't really happen in Norway. It would also be difficult given that organizations are typically as flat and horizontal as you are when intertwined in bed with a Norwegian, should you be so lucky.

DEALMAKING IN NORWAY

Who wants to buy a
Norwegian cabin?

Building trust

Norway is a country based on trust, and this is significantly important in the business world here. Trust is extensively woven throughout the entire society. A very simple example of this that in a city like Oslo you can leave your bag, your phone, or other valuables out in the open for extended periods of time, while in most other major cities such items would disappear quickly, likely never to be seen again. In Norway, there is a high level of trust for each other. Very few would steal someone's property or even disturb it anyway.

There is also a strong, and to some extent, blind trust for the government in Norway. As you can probably imagine, for an American this was difficult to adjust to. I mean, like any good American, I love my own country, I even love the government, but I absolutely do not trust them. Perhaps if you follow the news coming from America you can understand why. So, it has taken me some time to trust the government here in Norway. Although, one simply needs to look to the last few decades of how well the Norwegian government has taken care of its people. On top of that Norway was recently ranked the least corrupt country in the entire world. This is an incredible achievement when you consider that several other societies that have amassed their wealth from oil have not done so well to manage corruption. There's a reason to trust the government in Norway. You might even go as far as to say they're worth every krone they get from those ridiculously high tax rates.

Most shocking to a foreigner like myself is the trust that even large corporations have managed to build in Norway. I mean, trusting the government is one thing but a big scary corporation?!

This is so counter to both American and other global markets where big companies do big, bad things. Not so much in Norway. Here, people even love local airline companies! How often do you hear people speak fondly of an airline? Usually, it's more like complaints about rude service, delayed flights, and lost luggage. Having flown more miles than I care to admit between the US and Norway, I can tell you this is almost never the case. The planes are on time, my bags get where they should go, and the staff is not only nice but incredibly good looking. Corporations here operate differently. They care about their employees and customers. They won't do something bad for either party even if it means making slightly more profit. For this, and their typically squeaky clean history, they have earned the trust of the people.

On an individual level, most Norwegians consider themselves to be very trustworthy. They will feel great disrespect if you question their trustworthiness. This is important to know in business as many other business cultures do not operate this way. Instead, in those cultures, as you do business you set up many walls for protection and backup plans. You get lawyers to spin up endless terms that protect you in every obscure way possible. Or, you are always looking for some type of advantage as part of the deal. These types of moves will only concern a Norwegian. They will assume you don't trust them and as a result, they can't trust you. This will put an abrupt halt to your business dealings with them. I had to learn this lesson a few times the hard way.

Building trust in Norway takes a long time, so one has to prepare oneself to be patient. This applies to both personal and business relationships you'll make in the country. This can be one of the toughest things you'll encounter while doing business in Norway. It's common for outsiders to feel shut out or excluded while trying to build this elusive trust. This certainly doesn't help make the cold and dark winters any easier to manage. Just know that once you do build that trust, you can make a friend, a lover, or a business partner for life. Getting there, however, will be a foreigner's greatest challenge.

As a foreigner here in Norway, it's going to be an additional challenge to build this trust. While Norway is a very equal and inclusive country there is some distrust for outsiders here. Perhaps not by society as a whole, but more specifically in the business world. This is not going to be a popular sentiment, but this was my experience at least. The best I can figure is, it comes down to a few things. First, with Norway enjoying 50+ years of economic prosperity, there hasn't been much pressure to aggressively go global in business. Most businesses here do just fine selling only to the domestic market, especially where they have a monopoly position. So, the oil that has driven that prosperity is by far the largest export business. And since Norwegians prefer Norwegian products over, say, cheaper Chinese products, there's not much desire to do extensive importing, aside from importing a lot from Scandinavian neighbor countries who share a desire for quality products and similar aesthetics appeal. As a result, Norwegian businesses can sometimes lack experience working with foreigners.

On the rare occasion when I could get a Norwegian to be open to the challenge of working with foreigners, I sometimes got an interesting response. It was along the lines of "Oh yes, another American once came here for business and ripped a few people off" – they would say. When I would press for the American's name or which company they worked for, curiously the Norwegian could never remember. It's almost as if the story of a scary foreigner coming to Norway for business is a ghost tale, passed along throughout the years and likely starting with the discovery of oil and increased international interest in Norway. These stories have been used to scare generations of Norwegian workers from opening up themselves too much once independence was firmly established. You can see this further in Norway avoiding joining the EU on several occasions for example. Norwegians would rather do it themselves than be overly dependent or worse, in debt to an outsider.

That's not to say it's impossible to get a Norwegian to trust you as a foreigner here. I've managed to make it happen a few times, but more often than not, I've failed to establish the trust needed in business. Common reasons include being too aggressive, too impatient, but in most cases, it simply comes down to failing to understand Norwegians and their culture. However, when you do establish this trust you'll feel it. The typical Norwegian will start looking you in the eye and hanging on to your words instead of shying away. I wish you the best of luck in this regard – you'll need it.

How Norwegians manage risk

Norwegians manage risk in one very simple way: by trying to avoid it at all costs. OK, perhaps that's not entirely true, but it does sometimes feel this way as you start working with Norwegians. Getting them to try a new product, make a large business deal, or try a new business strategy will no doubt be one of your greatest challenges.

Strangely, this risk aversion doesn't apply to all facets of Norwegian society. No, the typical Norwegian will take great risks in nature for example. They will go on long extended hikes in the middle of nowhere and cross-country skiing in the very cold snow. They perch high above the daunting mountains that line the beautiful fjords, dangling their feet precariously. They jump in freezing lakes without much concern. And of course, after all those adventures they'll often consume alcohol at a rate that would send even the hardest partying American college kids to the hospital. This type of risk is encouraged in Norwegian society, even admired. However, things are a little different when it comes to risk in business.

Today in Norway, there is much talk about innovation. There is even a government organization called Innovation Norway focused solely on it. Ensuring Norwegian prosperity for the next 100+ years in the post-oil world is their key goal. There's just one big challenge when it comes to innovation in business: most companies, especially Norwegian companies, actually don't want it. They would much rather prefer the status quo and a profit margin that grows slowly over time instead. Innovation in business requires taking risk and that is something the Norwegian business culture is struggling with as of late.

I should know, as I work in what might be considered one of the riskiest forms of business, early stage technology startups and venture capital. Our industry is notorious for boom and bust cycles in addition to an incredibly high failure rate. The majority of these businesses (60%-80%) will completely fail, taking our investment money with them. It's only very rarely that you have a huge breakout success like Google or Facebook. Aside from those, there are countless dead bodies on the road to building a successful business. It's a model that works well in the liberal California industries, the opportunistic Chinese markets and tech savvy Israeli ecosystems, for example. In Norway, it has been a bit more difficult.

This is partly due to how the Norwegian economy works and their approach to extreme egalitarianism. If you are very successful in business the government will take much of that success in the form of extremely high tax rates. This is so that wealth can be redistributed to others who are perhaps not willing to take such risks to succeed. At the same time you have *Janteloven* (The Law of Jante), the cultural values that encourage Norwegians to not excel too far ahead of their peers. Serving as a weight upon the chest of the few Norwegian risk takers, it's a huge limitation of risk appetite here in Norway.

This can become challenging when conducting business here. Especially for an American like myself. We subscribe more to the theory of 'no risk, no reward'. To get the greatest reward, you often have to take the biggest risks in business. This is how many business cultures are taught: through tall tales of successful entrepreneurs that risked everything to make their mark.

Perhaps one of the greatest tales of taking risk in business concerns Elon Musk, the CEO of the electric car company Tesla. Earlier in his career he was a founder of PayPal, a successful financial technology company in Silicon Valley. When that company was sold, Elon managed to pocket $180M. Not bad! He then used those proceeds to put together new fledgling companies. He put $100M into SpaceX, $70M into Tesla, and $10M into SolarCity. Here's someone who made enough money to live comfortably for the rest of his life, perhaps on a warm beach somewhere with a drink in hand. Instead of resting, he immediately poured every dollar into three new innovative and extremely high-risk businesses. He likes to joke that at the time he even had to borrow money to pay his rent. That is the classic American risk taking attitude: putting it literally all on the line. Rolling the dice again and seeing what happens. You were lucky once so maybe it'll happen again. Norwegians are significantly less likely to do such a thing.

Even after a few years here, I have not managed to crack the code on how to get Norwegians to take more risks. Even worse, I can feel their lack of risk appetite starting to infect me. Although, I get it: life is good in Norway. Too good, actually! When everything is working so well, why take the chance to disrupt that? There's no pressure to take risks, and perhaps that's the root of the problem. If we think about how a diamond is created, it's done due to a whole lot of pressure forming this beautiful stone. The pressure in Norway is starting to increase, but today it's still a light and gentle push and perhaps not the crushing weight needed to drive impactful change. Let's hope that oil prices continue to fall, because as far as I see, that's the only thing starting to create some pressure here. With the amount of Tesla's you see on the streets in Norway, the future seems to indicate there won't be much need for the oil. In fact, the future is more likely to be found deep in software code versus deep in the ground. Along with that will be the need to take a few more risks.

Operating on Norwegian time

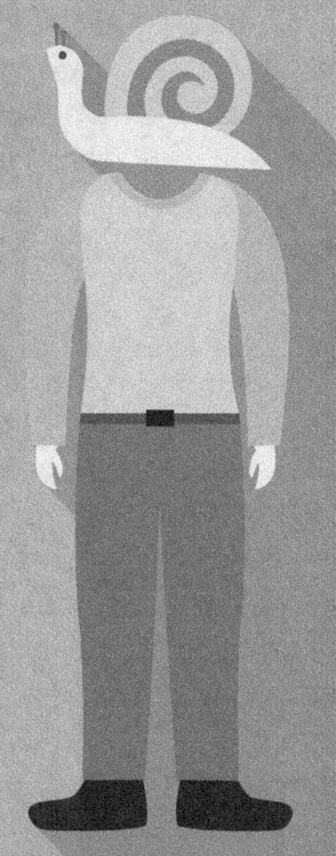

After spending enough time in Norway you might start to feel like time moves just a little slower here. Everyone and everything from planes to trains is on time, almost exactly on time in fact. Work is always delivered on time or as agreed upon. To not follow through on your word can cause you to lose trust in Norway. However, everything else just seems to take a little bit longer. The pace is noticeably subdued, and that's exactly how Norwegians like it. To rush something or haphazardly finish work is not the norm. To take an unnecessary shortcut to speed things up doesn't really happen here. Things get done when they get done. This doesn't help much when trying to do business deals with Norwegians. I soon learned how to operate on a whole new time scale: Norwegian time.

Now, this is when things get a little confusing. With Norwegian workers being so efficient in all the work they do, shouldn't things go faster? Let's just say like a certain relationship status on Facebook goes, it's complicated. The Norwegian is, yes, highly time efficient with their daily routines. Making deals and large advancements in business still take a great deal longer than it does in other business cultures.

One of my favorite examples of this is how Norwegians hyper-obsess over the design of just about any detail. No matter how small. I have on more than one occasion seen new products delayed because the color of a font was simply not quite right. It had to be rethought, discussed as a group, opened to people's opinions throughout the company, new samples reviewed and rethought again. Only then, after each detail has gone through this rigorous cycle could the team feel like it was ready to release. As you can imagine this dramatically reduces the speed of iteration cycles in Norwegian businesses.

Why are Norwegians like this? From my experience it comes down to two main things. The first is their concern that their product, their work, their contribution will not appeal to fellow Norwegians. If a product is not perceived as extremely high quality, borderline perfect, it's not likely to appeal to Norwegians. To release a product or service before every detail of it has been thoroughly scrutinized is simply too high of a risk for most Norwegians. They would rather not risk their reputation on something that is not perfect, or at least close to it.

Secondly, there is a rather high aversion to marketing and sales culture in Norway. Salespeople are considered to be less than trustworthy in this society. So there is a lot of reluctance to push your product out to the market until you're sure it's great. That includes not just the product itself, but every little design detail like the font used. It's hard enough for them to culturally proclaim their product is best, harder so when this longer process has not taken place.

In China you often hear the expression Chà bu duō (差不多) as you do business there. It roughly translates to "not much off" or "it's good enough". Order a new product and it's slightly the wrong size? It's good enough. Release a paper with a few typos? It's good enough. Building was built with slightly less floors than originally planned? It's good enough. While this attitude may not always produce the highest quality of results, it has allowed the Chinese to move exceptionally fast in business. It also allows them to fix problems with greater speed. Door keeps falling off its hinge? Get some used wire and a big nail, problem solved. You won't find much of this type of attitude in Norway.

Norwegians do have their own version of "it's good enough", "det er bra nok". However, it does not typically apply to producing business results faster or of lesser quality. It's more a comment that someone's work is good, but not great, although it still meets what some consider the low expectations of Norwegians. Remember, this is a culture that prefers to under promise on a business dealing, versus, say, the American approach of overpromising and being far too ambitious. If someone is only good enough in their job, they are not likely to be punished or replaced as would often happen in other business cultures. Excelling too far past your colleagues is also not normal here, so doing good-enough helps to keep everyone on a very level playing field when it comes to contribution in the workplace. In some cases, those who are great at their work will step in and to continue the work for those who are just good enough. Credit for the job will of course be shared equally across the team.

The final piece to working on Norwegian time includes a rather generous vacation schedule they receive. Norwegians will even take just about every religion's holiday off work, even though very few Norwegians are religious themselves. This, coupled with the Norwegian long summer holiday, can dramatically grind many business dealings to a halt. I've learned to be mindful of the calendar and upcoming holidays as it is related to closing deals and making progress on projects. It has been frustrating at times, especially in the fast moving business of technology startups where I work.

So grab a Snickers (or the local Norwegian favorite candy bar the *Kvikk Lunsj*) because it's going to take a while making business deals in Norway.

Negotiating techniques

There's probably only one thing Norwegians hate more than having to engage in small talk with their business colleagues. That is having to negotiate with them. The business culture here is typically more non-combative than found in other cultures, especially my dear old America, where we'll pretty much go to war over anything. During a difficult negotiation with a competitor, Apple founder Steve Jobs once famously replied he was "willing to go thermonuclear war on this". In Norway they tend to keep the warheads off the negotiation table and prefer to focus on finding a solution that is equally beneficial to both parties. Negotiation is approached more like joint problem solving: everyone should win.

Furthermore, in their deal making and negotiating, Norwegians are very transactional in nature. The deal must feel like both sides win and benefit equally. It has to be a 'win-win.' There is little affordance of one side getting preferential treatment, regardless of their status or reputation. In my industry of venture capital, one example of that is how ownership in the companies we invest in is allocated. In most other markets, investors like me receive 'preferred' shares because we are taking the majority of the risk. This gives us some additional rights and protections as part of the deal. The business owners receive 'common' shares even though they're doing the majority of the work. That type of lopsided deal doesn't work in Norway though. So here, I receive common shares just like everyone else. We're all equal, even when millions of dollars are on the line.

Norwegians approach negotiations in a pragmatic and logical method, usually in a simple list and top down format. As Norwegian negotiate they'll go through each condition one by one regardless of how large or small that condition may be in the grand scheme of things.

This can be frustrating for foreigners who are more accustomed to focusing on the larger deal points during a negotiation. This is, however, your chance to give concessions to the other side on smaller items of your deal. That allows you to further argue for your side on other deal points you feel are more important.

Negotiations should be simple to understand with all known information shared honestly within the group involved. Withholding information or misleading a Norwegian in any way will almost certainly cause a deal to break down. Any embellishing of information, data, or financials should never be done. You may find that Norwegians are not overly eager to share extensive information with you unprompted. They of course already have one of the best "poker faces" in the world thanks to their very stoic and Nordic appearances. Couple that with a lack of emotional reactions that certainly benefits them at the negotiation table.

There typically isn't extensive bargaining or haggling over prices. The Norwegians will tell you that only the Danes do that. As long as the price is considered fair, there will be very little wiggle room a Norwegian is willing to make. They are, however, usually more than able to make some compromises on other non-monetary deal points, as long as you also make similar and equal concessions. When a deal negotiation has reached a point that both parties have made equal sacrifices, it now has the opportunity to close.

Using highly aggressive sales tactics is never recommended when negotiating with Norwegians. In general, any type of conflict is never a good idea in Norway. These people are as peaceful as they are humble. To bully your way into a deal or attempt to intimidate the other side during a negotiation will almost certainly kill the deal.

Negotiating in Norway is not an emotional exercise, so raising your voice or losing your cool will cause a Norwegian to lose trust for you. It will also make them avoid engaging with you. And that's on top of how hard it already is to get them to talk to you!

I should take a moment to say that while Norwegians avoid aggression in business dealing, passive aggressiveness is a well loved national pastime. You could even say that Norwegians excel at being passive aggressive as much as they excel at cross-country skiing. They're pros! Expertly maneuvering their way through the workplace with subtle comments and smirks. Keeping up with technology, they have even managed to craft extremely passive aggressive online communications, hitting you with that subtle emoji at just the right time to emphasize how they're being a total prick or a bitch (known as a '*kjerring*' in Norwegian) but not overly rude.

There's a negotiation tactic that is popular in America and especially Silicon Valley where I'm from. We call it FOMO which stands for "Fear of Missing Out" and it's very effective. The concept is simple. I'm presenting you with an opportunity and if you don't jump on it right away, you'll have the fear that you missed out. This helps to drive some sense of urgency in a negotiation to push the deal along faster. I can tell you from personal experience, this hardly works in Norway. To attempt to rush a deal doesn't allow a Norwegian to thoroughly examine every detail and solicit the consensus needed in most Norwegian organizations.

Bringing up previously agreed to terms or aspects of a deal will make you appear to be untrustworthy. Once something has been agreed upon there is rarely room for reconsideration in Norwegian business culture. It's considered an inefficient use of time and Norwegians will want to avoid adding further complexity to something that is considered resolved. As we have previously discussed, Norwegians are very pragmatic people.

When the deal is done it should be easy for both parties to clearly walk away without additional attachments or risks. Trying to lock Norwegians into long term commitments, especially on your first negotiation, is not recommended. This will no doubt scare them away especially as it pertains to your first business deal with them. Trust and comfort with Norwegians is earned over time and dealings are well segmented between each other.

Norway is also one of the least corrupt countries in the world. So making bribes or even joking about them is never appropriate! This can be something as small as buying a business contact dinner. There is no concept of "greasing the wheels" with a bribe or favor as it exists in many other countries, especially emerging markets.

Contracts and the fine print

Norwegians are notoriously allergic to overly verbose contracts and extensive legal agreements. I learned this hard way over my years of doing business here. Upon arrival here I started by using the same type of legal documents I was accustomed to at home in America. These, I soon found out, were incredibly offensive to Norwegians, who in general feel like too much fine print shows a lack of trust. Since trust is the key pillar to Norwegian business, too much fine print is thought to erode that trust. This is also because legal English or legalese is difficult to understand even for native English speakers. Imagine how tough it is for those who have English as a second language.

Upon sending a rather simple consulting contract to a Norwegian business contact once:

"I'll get back to you soon on this. It may take me some time to digest the 'fine print' here". He passively aggressively replied in email.

The contract, especially by American standards, was rather light. It included two pages of the terms of our arrangement but also another two pages of the terms and conditions, aka the fine print. None of these terms would have been considered offensive in most other international business dealings but things are a little different in Norway. Since business is done on the basis of trust here, it's not recommended to over burden your business partners with extensive fine print. To do so can start your relationship off without this foundation of trust, making closing the deal and building further trust much more difficult.

In Norway, it's usually not required for a contract to be signed in person. As a fairly tech savvy population digital signatures are widely accepted. I have also received contracts that don't even require a signature. It's more of a statement of work between two parties. Once again, Norway is a country of trust so to not honor an agreement will quickly cause you to lose both authority and status in the business world here.

The art (and power)

of the handshake

A majority of the initial work I did in Norway consisted of fundraising capital: an incredibly difficult task in the country. Norwegians, despite their considerable wealth, are not overly eager to part with it, especially to a foreigner like myself. This is, of course, due in part to them being rather risk averse. Another reason is the incredibly high wealth taxes of the country. If I was successful with their investment money they'd have the luxury problem of owing an incredibly high amount come tax time. It's much safer to simply buy another house or cabin and leverage the tax benefits of such an investment. Finally, as a foreigner who just showed up in town asking for millions of dollars I could see how this might not be the most effective approach. Although in my previous home of Silicon Valley I saw this happen on a daily basis. As we have already learned trust is earned, and it takes time in Norway.

Once, after a successful meeting, I had done the impossible. I got a Norwegian to part with some of their money to support my project. We shook hands and parted our separate ways. I quickly, and somewhat frantically turned to my Norwegian colleague and said:

"We should get him a contract to sign ASAP to confirm his investment. Before he changes his mind!"

That's when she told me to relax. She further went on to say that we didn't need to worry. He shook on the deal and gave his word, something of significantly more importance in Norway than perhaps other business cultures.

In America, for example we shake on just about everything. But in terms of closing a deal, we often let the lawyers fight it out from that point. In America, and many other business cultures, a deal is never truly done until it's signed, usually on some overly detailed legal document. Things are however different in Norway. One's word and the handshake that accompanies it is incredibly symbolic.

It was also incredibly interesting to learn that an oral agreement can be legally binding in Norway. And most Norwegians believe this to be true, so they dare not violate it and risk a courtroom showdown. This is actually true in some other business cultures as well but it's not typically enforced. Most courts wouldn't hear something without more substantial proof or a legal document for reference. Norwegians however aren't eager to violate or even bend any potential law. So when they give you their word you can almost always believe it to be true.

WHY

NORWAY?

We opened this book talking about a phrase I heard often in Norway: "Welcome to Norway!" Used ironically the natives basically tried to help me understand some of the beautiful and odd peculiarities of their country while trying to help me join them in the fun. However there's a phrase, or more specifically, a question that a foreigner like myself will hear much more often here: "Why Norway?". Usually, that's also followed by "And do you plan to stay?". So much for feeling welcome.

These questions can easily be as jarring as the culture shock we foreigners sometimes experience in Norway. I didn't, and still to this day, understand completely why Norwegians often ask such questions. These questions are usually the first or second thing they ask you!

Norway is in fact a great country, a shining example for the rest of the world really of how to build and foster a society. This is a country that ranks incredibly high in terms of quality of life, equality and many more important dimensions. So when I hear this question I wonder why do Norwegians have such a lack of self confidence in themselves and their country? Is it really so hard to understand why someone would want to be here? At times it has even made me ask myself the very same questions. As a result it has often created a lot of personal conflict while I've tried to navigate and adapt to life in Norway.

There is of course no simple answer to these questions. For foreigners, your answers are obviously going to be unique to your own situation. Personally, I've tried many different answers with varying levels of success.

However the answer that I believe to be the most accurate is actually rather simple. Why Norway? Because I love Norway, and as part of that I want Norway to love me back. And this is a love that is not easy to obtain. But I know that through the struggles, the failures to adapt, and my many missteps it's going to be worth it. I believe this through-and-through not just for myself but for you, the reader as well whether you are Norwegian or a foreigner like myself. Because with increased collaboration and understanding of each other there's really no limit to what we can achieve together. Perhaps even one day these questions won't be so commonplace. Writing this book was the first step to such an ambitious goal.

Because I see such great business potential in Norway and Norwegians themselves. I hope you also can see that within these pages. As it was certainly not my intention to imply that Norwegians are bad at business or worse, impossible to work with. However to bridge our cultures, be it American to Norwegian or otherwise, both sides will need to adjust how we interact and perceive each other. That's going to take time. Even after a few years here in Norway I'm still learning, still making mistakes, and still on occasion being way too American. I try to make less mistakes each day and in the process, I'm getting closer to establishing this cultural bridge.

Along that journey of building this bridge there were, of course, many failures. My company didn't successfully expand to the Norwegian market. I managed to lose a fair amount of money for several parties, myself included. I drove a few relationships with Norwegians right into the ground, so much so that even to this day they avoid me in social or business settings. Despite all that I can however own up to those failures and face them head-on because that's what I was taught to do in Silicon Valley.

There the path to success is often dotted with many failures which is perfectly normal there. You might even say we embrace failure. After all, we like to say "You'll never hit a homerun if you don't take swing". It's more important to try and fail than to not try at all. As with each failure you'll become stronger and wiser. There's also always a second chance in America for redemption and to us success is the ultimate vindication of any previous wrongs.

And you could even say I'm literally in the business of failure. I work with early-stage startups where typically nine out of ten businesses fail. Over the years I've developed a rather tough skin when it comes to the subject. Often those businesses fail due to a failure to understand something. That might be something large, like how an entire industry works, but it can also be related to a failure to understand the many smaller nuances of a business. Death by a thousand papercuts, we like to say. This was also my experience with failure in Norway. It wasn't through any one specific action or inaction. Instead it was all these cultural nuances coming together to form a beautiful symphony of failure. And in Norway, a country of peace and quiet, even my loud instrument didn't make up for the fact that my approach was rather out of tune.

While this is not common in Norwegian society, I wear those business failures proudly on my sleeve and discuss them openly, mostly so others can benefit and learn from them. As I've discussed those failures with Norwegians a curious thing happened that gave me much hope. Often they would interrupt me – which is not a common thing for Norwegians to do! – and not allow me to categorize them as failures. They would say: "Sean, you absolutely did not fail. You challenged us and created an impact. For that we are grateful".

This was probably the nicest thing a Norwegian could ever say to me. And they were right because the same crazy new American business concepts I was trying to push forward are now being used by no less than five other Norwegian companies.

This is exactly how a society can benefit greatly from increased international collaboration. New ideas and new experiences help to foster new opportunities. New perspectives and new unions can build magic. There's an English word that well encapsulates this and the word itself even sounds a bit magical. It's a word that you don't often hear in Norway as there is probably no good Norwegian translation for it. That word is serendipity. It suggests that through chance encounters or developments something great can happen. However for serendipity to happen you have to have an open mind and, more importantly, open eyes lest you miss the opportunity for it even when it's right in front of your face.

Let's get back to that other question I'm often asked: "Do you plan to stay?" The truth is I could leave tomorrow or in 10 years. It doesn't really matter in the end. The Norwegian experience will always be with me and part of me forever. It has left an indelible mark on how I perceive the world and my place in it. I now simply see this question as more of a test from Norwegians. Trying to determine both my own strength and loyalty to this great country. Because as we've previously discussed one must suffer and struggle here in Norway to earn the great honor of calling this country home. So I now use my answer more as an opportunity to catch the inquisitive Norwegian off guard. Answering with either "Yes I love it here! Amazing weather!" or "Yes, I'm thinking about getting on your welfare system and riding that out for as long as possible!"

Neither answer wins me much favor but I enjoy introducing Norwegians to the great American pastime that is sarcasm. They almost never pick up on it and that's perfectly alright.

Different cultures may never be able to truly understand one another. However, we still have much to share with each other. And Norway has much to share with you. The country is opening up to us foreigners despite the perceived walls that may appear to be in the way. I hope these pages have served as a metaphorical ladder to help you climb them. For you Norwegians out there, I hope these same pages have opened your eyes to the challenges us foreigners sometimes have climbing those walls. This book is my humble contribution to help us meet at the top of that wall. The view up here can be as breathtaking as any fjord.

It's not going to be easy to climb that wall however, Norwegians will want to keep pushing you down as you try, driving you down to the same level as them if you dare to be bold and pop your head above what's considered acceptable. They'll push you down and try to force you to become just like them. I encourage you to not let them be successful in doing so. Yes, you must adjust, both your perception and how you conduct yourself here in this society. At times you'll have to step down a little in order to satisfy them. But regardless of where you come from, you have something to share with Norwegians. You'll learn a lot from them but ensure they are also learning from you and from the rich history of your own culture.

So please allow me to answer that first question in the most American way possible.

Why Norway?

Because why the hell not?

—Welcome to Norway.

GLOSSARY

Here's a few words you might hear as you work with Norwegians. Pull one out to impress a colleague sometime!

BIRKEBEINERRENNET – A famous ski race in Norway that business executives often participate in. Companies have their own teams and your achievement in the tracks has become as important as your resume.

DET GRØNNE SKIFTET – 'The Green Shift'. Creating a sustainable society based on green jobs and reducing the country's dependency on oil and gas production.

FELLESFERIE – The summer holiday shutdown. You won't be getting much work done this time as your colleagues will no doubt be out on holiday.

FJORD – One Norwegian word that has become truly international. Fjord in its basic meaning 'where one fares through' has the same origin as the word "fare" (travel) and the noun "ferry". The narrow canyons with steep sides called fjords are formed by giant glaciers slowly moving across the land and carving these paths.

GÅ PÅ TUR – 'Take a hike!' Literally. Not everybody actually does it, but everybody likes to give the impression they do it, and everybody at the very least talks about it. Norwegians love exercise!

HV-ØVELSER – Similar to the American National Guard, this is a mandatory military training exercise some of your colleagues might be part of. It's the one time when it's OK to make jokes about shooting guns with a Norwegian.

HYTTE – A small winter or summer cabin that Norwegian workers like to retreat to as much as possible. In Norwegian business culture it's not considered extravagant to have a cabin.

KVIKK LUNSJ – The Norwegian version of a Kitt-Katt bar. You eat these with your Norwegian colleagues after a good cross country ski. Norwegians just love milk chocolate!

LANGRENN – Cross country skiing is a long and tiring physical activity your Norwegian colleagues will try to talk you into. A Norwegian will tell you that cross-country skiing involves the highest endurance levels of all sports, as its motions make use of every major muscle group, and that it burns the most calories. So in other words it's pure torture.

Typical Norwegians You'll Meet in the Workplace

These are not meant to resemble any specific Norwegians I've worked with, mostly because Norway is a small country and I'm likely to see these people often!

That all being said, here are some very broad generations of Norwegians you'll meet while working in Norway.

Recognize anyone?

Typical Norwegian Businessman

The typical Norwegian or den typiske nordmann, is the proudest Norwegian you'll meet. He's proud of his country and proud of his cross-country skiing. He's also incredibly proud of that one time he was successful in business 20 years ago and hasn't stopped talking about it since. He's a global traveler but skeptical of foreigners who come to Norway for business. He feels that business in Norway is best done by and with other Norwegians.

Miss Follow Through

They are your modern empowered Norwegian businesswoman. She enjoys one of the smallest gender pay gaps in the world thanks to Norway's emphasis on fairness and equal pay. She's known in the office for always following through on her work, which earns her great respect. That's due to her approach of under-promising and over delivering to her colleagues.

The Love Refugee

Not a native Norwegian but an expat who settled in Norway many years ago. Like most foreigners who settle here, they came here for love. The rather attractive Norwegians have managed to keep a steady flow coming here which is really great. As the cold weather is almost tolerable when you have a warm body next to you. For a foreigner, they will be much easier to get to know on both a personal and business level. They understand how challenging it can be to form relationships here in Norway.

Mr Gotta Go

A slippery one, they are the most difficult Norwegian to get to know either personally or on a business level. A master of slipping away to avoid small talk or business dealings, they are a tricky one to connect with. Look for opportunities to connect over a hobby like skiing or doing dugnad (community work) away from the office.

That One Loud Guy

One of the few loud voices you'll find in Norway, they don't respect the quiet sanctuary of the Norwegian office. They are known for squawking at meetings and around the office, much to the dismay of coworkers who prefer more peaceful surroundings. When Norwegian drinking culture comes into play, that loudness only intensifies with each shot of aquavit they consume.

The Ol' Polar Bear

It's been a rough few years for polar bears and not just because of global warming! His job as a janitor is perhaps considered less prestigious from a foreigner's view, but in Norway, thanks to flat hierarchies and extreme egalitarianism, his contribution is valued by society at the same level as the others. The Norwegian state supplies healthcare and a financial safety net to him regardless of his presence in a lower tax bracket.

Super Sporty Scandie

They never stop moving and live a very healthy lifestyle. They will almost always be planning a hike, going skiing, swimming in a fjord, or just doing any other physical activity. They are super sporty and as a result, have exceptionally low BMI (and typically a very cute butt). They also don't let work get in the way when the weather is nice, or physical activity can take them out of the office. Your best chance to catch them and build a relationship will be to join her or him in one of these physical activities. If they see a foreigner embrace Norwegian nature and exercise, this can help you earn their great respect.

Tall, Blond, and Millennial

This friendly and eager millennial is just entering the Norwegian workforce. Raised in a highly functional and fair socially democratic society, their optimism can only be matched by their drive to do good in the world. They are less held back by the restrictive Law of Jante and as a result, represent great potential for Norway's future. Now, if we could only get them to stop constantly staring at their phones.

The Old Timer

The old-timer has seen it all before and isn't interested in doing business differently. Especially when that new approach is proposed by a foreigner. They will be most skeptical and address the outsider with an uninterested response, followed by the exhibition of a general lack of willingness to work together.

No Plan too Small

They create a plan for the plan and backup plans for both plans. They book meetings to plan a future meeting. They can whip up a plan with great speed because Norwegians take great pride in being able to do such an exercise. The output is generally considered less important than planning for the output itself.

Special thanks to the following people who helped shape both this book in addition to my Norwegian experience.

Sondre for his fabulous insights and unique perspective into Norwegian society and its history.

Dan for his comedic stylings and being my favorite fellow expat.

Haakon, Anders, Tharald, Ida, MK, Per-Martin, Bela, Sagar and Nina my Norwegian colleagues who probably assumed most of this book would be about them.

Simon for the sauna sessions and for getting me to jump into the freezing cold Oslo fjord my first (and perhaps last) time.

Neil for being my favorite brit to share a pint and a karaoke duet with.

Dave, my former boss, for giving me the chance to expand our business to Norway, as crazy as that sounded at the time.

Stina for being the first Norwegian to trust me and for helping me see the true beauty of Norway.

*I dedicate this book to Nanny, who gave me the name
'The Loud American' and reminds me to never
stop roaring loud like a lion.*

Need more help Working with Norwegians?

Scan to buy

Get the companion book to this one, *Living with Norwegians*

Available at
www.livingwithnorwegians.com

ISBN: 9788269237986

Thanks for reading the book. In the spirit of the book and "pay it forward" culture, I encourage you to give the book to someone else who is new to Norway. Before you do that, sign your name below.

Name \ Where are you from?   Date

_________________________________   __________

_________________________________   __________

_________________________________   __________

_________________________________   __________

_________________________________   __________

_________________________________   __________

New to Norway Pro Tip:

Bookis Marketplace

Use Bookis.com to resell this book and even get a chance to meet up with other book-loving Norwegians. Scan the QR code to get started.

bookis.com